ENGLISH FOR BUSINESS SUCCESS

MAKING BUSINESS DECISIONS

Real Cases from Real Companies

FRANCES BOYD

American Language Program,
Columbia University

Longman

Making Business Decisions:
Real Cases from Real Companies

Credits appear on page 163.

Acquisitions director: Joanne Dresner
Development editor: Penny Laporte
Production editor: Nik Winter
Text design: A Good Thing
Cover design: Curt Belshe
Cover photos: Akzo, n.v.; Johnson & Johnson Consumer Products, Inc.;
    The Boeing Company; Ben & Jerry's Homemade, Inc.
Production supervisor: Anne Armeny

Library of Congress Cataloging-in-Publication Data

Boyd, Frances Armstrong.
    Making business decisions : real cases from real companies /
Frances Boyd.
        p.   cm.
    ISBN 0-201-59281-9
        1. Decision-making—Problems, exercises, etc. 2. Industrial
management—Problems, exercises, etc. 3. English language—Business
English—Problems, exercises, etc. 4. English language—Textbooks
for foreign speakers.   I. Title.
HD30.23.B68   1994
658.4'03—dc20
                                                            93-34169
                                                            CIP

12131415-VG-04 03 02 01

*To Alejandro and Eduardo
whose conception roughly paralleled that of this book
and whose adaptability made the project possible.*

ACKNOWLEDGMENTS

I want to thank all of the individuals at all of the companies who responded to my many requests for information, photos, permissions, and interviews. In many ways, a book of this nature depends on their good will and on their belief in the educational value of the project.

I want to thank my colleagues at the American Language Program, especially Patrick Aquilina, Tess Ferree, Gail Fingado, Jane Kenefick, Barbara Miller, Judy Miller, Carol Numrich, and Shelley Saltzman, for trying out, clarifying, and generally improving these cases.

I also want to thank our many students at the American Language Program who worked enthusiastically with these materials.

Special thanks to:
Dr. Robert M. Anderson, for advice on negotiating strategies, meeting management, and business writing.

John Behan, Esq., for help with legal research.

Mr. Theodore Teplow, for help with research on the valve market in Latin America.

Deborah and Peter Roth, for their willingness to share information about their lives and their livelihood.

Professors Kirby Warren and James Kuhn of the Columbia University School of Business for inspiration on the case method and thoughts on business ethics.

Penny Laporte, Development Editor, for insight, patience, and encouragement throughout the writing and editing process.

Joanne Dresner, Acquisitions and Development Director, for vision and encouragement throughout the project.

Carlos Velázquez, for the myriad sacrifices required to keep family life functioning in the face of a project of unknowable proportions.

CONTENTS

TO THE TEACHER

Overview

Making Business Decisions is a book and audiotape intended for learners of English who have business careers or want to prepare for business careers, as well as for those who simply want to know more about business. It is suitable for language courses in educational and work settings. No special knowledge of business is required. If you or the students have a business background, however, such knowledge can enhance class discussions.

The purpose of the book is to help students learn to communicate, in English, like business managers and feel confident doing so. To accomplish this goal, the book presents ten cases that put students into the shoes of real executives in multinational and U.S. companies. Each case contains discussion, reading, vocabulary, and writing activities, as well as a section on either listening or using charts and graphs. Particular attention is given to developing such business skills as quickly gathering and interpreting data from a variety of sources (photos, charts, interviews, press and business reports, colleagues); using culturally appropriate negotiating strategies; leading and participating in effective business meetings; writing clear, concise letters and proposals; and making intelligent business decisions based on data, experience, cultural sensitivity, and common sense.

The business issues in the cases include timely and significant questions about expanding internationally, negotiating international trade agreements, and responding to environmental concerns. The cases involve operations in the United States, Europe, Japan, and Latin America. The companies in the book make products ranging from airplanes to ice cream. Some of the firms are very large, some are medium-sized, and some are small. All of them are successful. And, they are successful because their executives make thoughtful decisions day after day as they face complex situations.

Encourage students to read and listen to business news. Help them draw parallels to the cases they are studying. Undoubtedly, they will hear about other companies in many parts of the world that are facing similar issues.

Suggestions for Use

The activities in *Making Business Decisions* are organized into cases: real situations faced by the busy and talented executives who run these ten companies. Each unit has material for four to six hours of classroom study. The cases can be studied in any sequence. Do note, however, that introductory lessons on business writing appear in Units Two and Three and the more complex cases appear in the second half of the book. You may choose to expand the cases with complementary work on presentation skills or pronunciation. Guest talks by business people in the community or visits to nearby firms can also complement the book's focus on real companies and the executives who run them.

The case materials are flexible. They can be used with small or large groups and with students who have a great deal of or very little business experience. You will want to vary the approach to suit your students and to maintain their interest.

Part One: Background

Examining the Products
Students look at information and photos from a real company. Then they discuss a few questions in order to familiarize themselves with the products and some of the business issues. Work as a whole class or break up into small groups, especially if the class is large. Generally ten to fifteen minutes is adequate for this activity.

Exercise 2—Gathering Data

Here students continue to build up their store of data about the company. In six units, they listen to interviews with executives who give background information and personal opinions about the company. By answering information questions (Part A) and reflection questions (Part B), students get a feel for the company and for how these successful managers approach their work. In two units, students use questionnaires to practice market research techniques, using the class as a sample. In the two remaining units, students practice reading data from charts and graphs related to the case. All of these work well as paired activities, and take twenty to thirty minutes.

Exercise 3—Gathering Data: Reading

In this three-part activity, students greatly expand their knowledge of the background of the company and of the specific issue they will later discuss at a business meeting (Exercise 6).

In **A. Scanning for Information,** students are asked to scan for, note down, and share detailed information from press articles and research reports. Have them work in groups of two or three. Call their attention to the model notes in the first two units and help them practice taking short, clear notes, focusing on the specific data required by the outline. If some students finish before others in their group, they can begin reading the other articles. To save time or vary the approach, you may want to ask students to complete this part of the activity outside of class. In class, allow fifteen to twenty minutes for reading and taking notes. Then, have students share the vital information on their outlines with their group members (who have read different articles). As they listen, students fill in their outlines completely. Allow fifteen to twenty minutes for this data sharing. As their skills develop, students will be able to scan, take notes, and share data more quickly.

In **B. Interpreting Information,** students are asked to use their completed outlines to make inferences about business issues in the company. They are given statements with which to agree or disagree or questions to discuss. Work in groups or as a whole class. Encourage those who have worked in or studied business to share their knowledge. Allow ten to fifteen minutes for this activity.

In **C. Reviewing Background Information and Vocabulary,** students focus on idioms and other common expressions used earlier in the unit. The items are embedded in sentences that review background information about the company and its executives. This short activity can be done outside of class.

Part Two: Decision Making

Exercise 4—Exploring Business Culture

As preparation for the business meeting (Exercise 6), this activity presents either a checklist of business practices or a short reading about one particular practice essential to the case. Topics include business ethics, copyrights and trademarks, and employer-employee relations. Encourage students to share their experience and to discuss the business practices in light of their cultural perspective. The reading can be done at home or in class. Allow fifteen to twenty minutes for the in-class discussion in small groups.

Exercise 5—Strategies for Negotiation

Also as preparation for the business meeting, students are given a negotiating strategy, the language they need to employ it, and a short, fun exercise to practice the strategy in small groups or pairs. Such negotiating strategies as conceding a point, inventing possibilities, and interrupting for clarification are included. Urge students to list the strategies and expressions on cards, build up a personal collection of cards and use them at each business meeting (Exercise 6). A list of strategies and expressions from all ten units is provided in Appendix B for reference.

This exercise helps students identify and use culturally appropriate negotiation strategies. Many of these are sophisticated strategies with deep cultural overtones, so students may want to discuss the cultural differences and their reactions to them. Allow fifteen to twenty minutes for this activity.

Exercise 6—Conducting a Business Meeting

This activity puts students at the center of the decision-making process. It calls on them to use all of the information, vocabulary, and skills from the unit to discuss and make decisions regarding such major business issues as opening foreign markets, responding to environmental concerns, and paying employees fairly.

In **A. Preparing for the Meeting,** students review the business problem and the format of the meeting. Urge them to review the background data, vocabulary, business culture information, and negotiating skills from the whole unit. The better informed they are, the more productive the meeting will be. Each student-run meeting is carefully structured to include an introduction, an agenda, and a closing. This preparation activity can be done outside of class.

In **B. Conducting the Meeting,** students choose who will run the meeting and who will take which roles. Alternatively, you can assign roles and have students prepare them outside of class. In large classes, students can be assigned to present specific points from the role summaries. During the business meeting, students analyze the problem (What's wrong?) and suggest alternative courses of action (What can we do about it?). Here, too, those with business experience or theoretical knowledge can contribute their expertise. The cases present opportunities to participate in meetings with consultants, customers, competitors, and one's own colleagues and staff.

The structure and purpose of the meetings may present strong cultural differences for some students. Seize the opportunity to have students identify and discuss these differences. The meeting may take from thirty-five to fifty minutes. To give feedback on language, negotiating strategies, and meeting management, you may want to take notes or to record some meetings on audio- or videotape.

Exercise 7—Follow-Up Activities

In **A. Business Writing,** students practice communicating their business decisions and ideas in letters, interoffice letters, and business proposals. Units Two and Three contain introductory material that asks students to analyze the form and content of business letters and interoffice letters, or memos. Depending on their backgrounds, they may find cultural and stylistic differences. From time to time, you may want to analyze student samples of business writing in class. The writing activity itself can be done outside of class.

In **B. Putting the Problem in Perspective: Applying Business Concepts,** students read a summary of the specific case. This denser, more difficult text incorporates vocabulary from the entire unit. It places the particular case in a more general context. Concepts that have been introduced throughout the unit are highlighted in the text. First, students are asked to react to the summary in a global way. Then, they are asked to answer questions, using the highlighted business vocabulary in their answers. Those with business experience may have stories to tell. You may want to use this as a closing exercise. Or, you may want to return to it later as a review.

Some units also include a part **C,** which is either authentic documents from the company presented for discussion or fieldwork assignments in which students are asked to explore the business community nearby.

Concluding Thoughts

I hope that the cases in *Making Business Decisions* will help students develop the skills, knowledge, cultural sensitivity, and confidence they need in order to conduct business anyplace where English is the international language of business. Beyond this, I hope that the cases let you and your students sense some of the excitement and challenge of working in today's global business world.

KENTUCKY FRIED CHICKEN CORPORATION

Adapting to the Japanese Market

Unit

1

BACKGROUND

1. Examining the Products

Read the information and look at the photographs in order to become familiar with Kentucky Fried Chicken (KFC) and some of its products. Then answer the questions.

Kentucky Fried Chicken Corporation

- Has its headquarters at 1441 Gardiner Lane
                              Louisville, Kentucky 40232.
- Was founded in 1955.
- Has 4,500 restaurants in the United States and 1,000 outside the United States, mostly in Australia, Britain, and Japan.

This is a typical KFC outlet in a U.S. suburb. The restaurant occupies its own building and has a standard size and design. Colonel Sanders, whose picture appears in all of the restaurants, is the founder of KFC.

Here is a "finger lickin' good" meal from a KFC restaurant in the United States. It includes chicken, cole slaw, mashed potatoes with gravy, soda, and a biscuit.

This is a menu from a KFC outlet in Japan.

1. Why are KFC restaurants popular? Consider, for example, service, image, quality, taste, price, and convenience.
2. Are there KFC or other fast-food chicken restaurants in your city or hometown?

2. Gathering Data: Using a Questionnaire

The questionnaire that follows asks for the kind of information KFC executives could use to determine promising locations for new restaurants.

A.   Use the questionnaire to find out about your classmates' eating habits and attitudes toward restaurants. Answer the questions; then work in pairs. Ask your partner the questions and take notes on the responses.

Eating Habits and Consumer Attitudes: Fast-Food and Other Restaurants

	You	Your Partner
1. How often do you eat restaurant food rather than home cooking? Have your habits changed recently? Why?		
2. Do you eat in fast-food restaurants (for example, KFC or McDonald's)? If so, how often? If not, why?		
3. Do you eat breakfast, lunch, dinner, or snack in fast-food restaurants?		
4. Do you think that fast-food is junk food (high-calorie, low-nutrition food) or healthy food?		
5. When you travel, do you patronize fast-food restaurants? Why or why not?		
6. Do you order take-out food? If so, how often? If not, why?		

B.   Discuss your reactions to the answers on the questionnaire. Did anything surprise or interest you particularly? What do the responses tell you about consumer eating habits?

3. Gathering Data: Reading

Kentucky Fried Chicken is a large international company with restaurants in several countries. Among KFC's most successful business plans was its decision to enter the Japanese market.

Read these articles to gather background data on this decision, including information to answer these questions:

- How did KFC analyze Japan as a market for fast food?
- What marketing strategy did KFC use to enter the Japanese market?

Work in groups of three. Look at the KFC-Japan Fact sheet on page 6. Each person should scan one of the three articles and take notes in the appropriate section of the outline. Then, share information so that everyone in your group has the same data and can fill in the KFC-Japan Fact Sheet completely.

1. JAPAN AS A FAST-FOOD MARKET

Fast food was not common in Japan when Kentucky Fried Chicken decided to enter the market. The company saw a promising business opportunity and found ways to overcome potential obstacles.

Japan is a rich, populous country of some 120 million, 90 percent of whom consider themselves middle class. It is thus the second largest consumer economy in the world, outranked only by the United States itself. The Japanese are well disposed toward[1] U.S. citizens and their products; Western models and celebrities, for example, appear frequently in Japanese advertising. . . .

Japan is the restaurant capital of the world, with one eating establishment for every eighty-one people. In recent years, with income rising and leisure time more plentiful, the industry has boomed. Fast food in particular has proved inordinately popular, growing by a factor of six[2] in the last ten years. . . .

Kentucky Fried Chicken began its Japanese operation with two test operations, one at Expo in Osaka, the other in a Tokyo department store. The company had a good product to offer: Chicken is popular in Japan anyway, and KFC's chicken tasted a little like *yakitori*, the broiled chicken on a stick that is one of Japan's most popular dishes. Still, the experiments were successful beyond all expectations. The Expo outlet broke records[3]: Sales there reached $100,000 a month.

Shortly thereafter KFC set up a fifty-fifty joint venture[4] with Mitsubishi, the giant Japanese trading company. Mitsubishi could guide KFC through the Japanese bureaucracy, making sure it complied with[5] applicable laws and followed appropriate customs. In addition, a year before, Mitsubishi had bought heavily into the chicken feed and farm business. Now, it gave KFC access to well-developed sources of supply. And it had an interest of its own. It could sell its chickens to KFC, which would be only too delighted to have a reliable supply.

SOURCE: *Enterprise.* Eric Sevareid. 1984. McGraw-Hill, N.Y. Used by permission.

1. tend to like
2. six times its original size
3. did better than before
4. a company 50 percent owned by Mitsubishi and 50 percent owned by KFC (United States)
5. obeyed

2. KFC-JAPAN MARKETING STRATEGY: PART ONE

Kentucky Fried Chicken has enjoyed a great deal of success in the Japanese market. Loy Weston, who was in charge of KFC-Japan, hired Shin Okuhara, his Japanese executive vice president, to help him tune in to the Japanese way of doing business. Their strategy worked well: Within eleven years, 324 KFC outlets had opened in Japan. Of these, 125 were directly run by the company and 199 were franchises, owned by individuals who had bought a license from KFC....

Kentucky Fried Chicken has muscled[1] its way into the number-one spot in Japanese fast food.... Its success, however, probably has less to do with luck than with good management and astute marketing.

One step in the marketing strategy is determining store location. Where a typical KFC outlet in the United States is freestanding—and thus built to the same size and specifications everywhere—the typical Japanese store is located in an existing building. Many are smaller than KFC's standard size. "What we do is design a store appropriate for Japan," explained Weston. "Every time we find a little space, we design a way to fit our store in. We shrink equipment, redesigning it, making it taller instead of longer." Kentucky Fried Chicken's outlets may be only one-third the size of U.S. prototypes,[2] but they do twice the business, an average of $620,000 a year.

Because the rent is high in Japan, sites have to be selected with particular care. To qualify for consideration a district must have at least 50,000 people using its train station every day. The number of people fifteen minutes away by bus or by foot is computed, and the number of passersby per hour is multiplied by store frontage, to produce something called the location factor. Then all these figures are fed into a formula designed to estimate sales....

As in other countries, KFC varied the menu to accommodate local tastes. "The Japanese aren't thrilled about mashed potatoes and gravy, which are common in both the United States and Australia," Weston said, "so we switched to french fries." When Japanese consumers found the cole slaw (cabbage salad) too sweet, KFC cut the sugar in half. The company catered to Japanese preferences in other ways, too. Smoked chicken, yogurt, and fish and chips, for example, all adorn KFC's Japanese menus.

1. aggressively pushed
2. models

KFC-Japan Fact Sheet

1. Japan as a Fast Food Market

A. Opportunities for KFC

   1. Population
120 million

   2. Wealth
90% middle class

   3. Attitudes toward U.S. products

   4. Restaurant industry

   5. Popularity of chicken

B. Obstacles for KFC to Overcome

   1. Laws

   2. Customs

   3. Source of chicken

2. KFC-Japan Marketing Strategy: Part One

A. Store Location

   1. Type of building
existing building

   2. Size of store
1/3 size of U.S. store

   3. Site selection

B. Menu Adaptions

   1. Potato

   2. Cole slaw

   3. Added items

3. KFC-Japan Marketing Strategy: Part Two

A. Advertising

   1. On-site strategies
models of food in display cases
life-size statue of Colonel Sanders

   2. TV advertising

B. Training

   1. Employee training: type and purpose

   2. Franchise development: type and purpose

C. Local Traditions

   1. Personal selling

   2. Local superstitions

3. KFC-JAPAN MARKETING STRATEGY: PART TWO

Loy Weston, head of KFC-Japan, and Shin Okuhara, his Japanese executive vice president, planned the company's entry into the market with great care. As restaurants were added, they continued to run some, but many were run by Japanese franchisees, people who had bought licenses from KFC. From the central office, Weston and Okuhara directed efforts in advertising, training, and adapting to local traditions....

Two devices—one dictated by Japanese custom, the other a brainchild of Weston's—marked KFC's on-site promotional strategy. Every restaurant in Japan displays models of the food it serves in glass display cases near the door.... Factories specializing in manufacturing the models ... provided KFC with a thirteen-piece set of chicken for eighty-five dollars each. Every store had to have one.

Every store also got a life-size statue of Colonel Sanders himself to put on the sidewalk outside the door. These were Weston's idea. ... Respected brand names and authenticity are highly valued in Japan, and the move made KFC outlets instantly recognizable.

Kentucky Fried Chicken in Japan spends $5 million a year on television commercials alone. The account is handled by a joint venture, this one between a Japanese advertising firm and the <u>McCann-Erickson agency</u>.[1]

Another aspect of the company's marketing effort is its extensive training of employees. When they start, they get nine days of basic operation training and four days of on-the-job training.... The purpose of the training is not only to develop skills but also to create company loyalty. Every morning KFC employees all over Japan repeat the company <u>pledge</u>.[2] The franchisees, who pay KFC a $10,000 licensing fee plus 4 percent of their yearly gross, are similarly imbued with company spirit, though in a more relaxed atmosphere. Every year they are invited to an elegant restaurant, at company expense, the night of the annual KFC convention. The

$9,000 this event costs is considered a worthwhile expense.

Before opening a restaurant, the Japanese pursue a well-established strategy of personal selling. <u>Capitalizing on</u>[3] the social nature of much of Japanese business, KFC representatives pay calls on local merchants in the neighborhood around an outlet. The store's managers introduce themselves to the other businessmen, offering gifts of smoked chicken and discount coupons for opening day....

Beyond its marketing expertise KFC had one more <u>asset</u>[4] apparently working for it: local superstition. "KFC's buildings are shaped like <u>pagodas</u>,"[5] Weston explains, "and our company colors are red and white, Japan's national colors that stand for happiness. And we usually try to open our new stores on one of the twelve lucky days in the Japanese calendar. Once, because three is a lucky number, we opened three stores on March 3, the third day of the third month."

---

1. a well-known U.S. advertising agency
2. statement of responsibility
3. taking advantage of
4. advantage
5. religious buildings of the Far East

B. Interpreting Information

Review the information in your KFC-Japan Fact Sheet. Read each statement below. Decide whether you agree or disagree with it. Write *agree* or *disagree* in the blank. Work in small groups. Compare your answers with those of a classmate, and explain your opinions. There is no one right answer.

_____ 1. The KFC expansion into Japan was not very risky because there were more opportunities than obstacles in the market.

_____ 2. The modifications in the KFC store design for the Japanese market were very minor.

_____ 3. A KFC-Japan menu would not be popular anywhere else.

_____ 4. The on-site and TV advertising strategies for KFC-Japan would also be appropriate for a number of other countries.

_____ 5. Executives of KFC-Japan were clever in using local traditions to help their business.

C. Reviewing Background Information and Vocabulary

Read the sentences and find the word or expression in the box that means the same as the italicized words. Then compare your answers with those of a classmate. If you disagree, consult another classmate, a dictionary, or your teacher.

a. retail stores

b. aggressively pushed

c. did better than before

d. be customers of

e. restaurant food packaged to take home to eat

f. change

g. six times larger

h. growing rapidly

i. obey

j. is larger than

_____ 1. The Japanese economy has grown dramatically over the last generation. It now *outranks* the economies of many nations in the world.

_____ 2. Kentucky Fried Chicken saw a big opportunity in the Japanese market: The economy was *booming* and chicken was a favorite food already.

_____ 3. Loy Weston, head of KFC-Japan, thought he might get Japanese consumers to *switch* from chicken yakitori, broiled chicken on a stick, to crispy Kentucky Fried Chicken.

_____ 4. Weston hired Shin Okuhara, a Japanese printing and paper executive who had hoped to do business with KFC. Okuhara helped the U.S. executive design Japanese KFC *outlets* that would appeal to the local customers.

_____ 5. Kentucky Fried Chicken also cooperated with Mitsubishi, a large trading company that owned many chicken farms. Mitsubishi executives helped Weston *comply with* Japanese laws.

_____ 6. To get local people to *patronize* KFC, Weston decided that the restaurants should include such familiar sights as models of food in the window.

_____ 7. Although the original KFC restaurants in the United States had sold mostly *take-out*, the ones in Japan were designed mainly as eat-in restaurants.

_____ 8. The Weston-Okuhara marketing strategy was a success. Several of the restaurants attracted huge numbers of customers and *broke records.*

_____ 9. Kentucky Fried Chicken was part of a general growth in fast-food restaurants in Japan. During KFC's early years, the fast-food business there grew *by a factor of six.*

_____10. Kentucky Fried Chicken *muscled* its way to the top of the Japanese fast-food industry by adapting its marketing to the Japanese business environment, hiring Japanese executives, and setting up joint ventures with Japanese firms.

PART 2

MAKING DECISIONS—ADAPTING TO INTERNATIONAL MARKETS

Introduction to the Problem. Competition in the fast-food chicken business is increasing all over the world. Kentucky Fried Chicken's adaptation strategy has been so successful in Japan that the company wants to use its experience elsewhere. The problem is to find new KFC countries and new locations within existing KFC countries.

Keep the problem in mind as you do the following exercises.

4. Exploring Business Culture: Franchising

Read the information. Work in small groups to answer the questions.

Franchising is a form of business ownership that is used by KFC and is becoming more common in many industries and countries.

Most KFC restaurants are franchises: They are owned by independent operators (franchisees) who buy a license from the company (franchisor) to open a restaurant at a specific location. With the license, franchisees purchase the right to use a corporate identity and corporate design: The image of KFC as well as the particular packaging, store design, and way of preparing chicken associated with the company. KFC franchisees are required to pay the parent company an initial fee of several thousand dollars and monthly fees of about 4 percent of their gross (pretax) sales. In addition, they must contribute 1.5 percent of gross sales to a company fund for advertising and use 3 percent of their gross sales for local promotion.

For entrepreneurs without a lot of money or business experience, franchises offer many advantages. The U.S. Small Business Administration estimates that 65 percent of new businesses in the United States fail within five years, whereas fewer than 5 percent of franchise-owned outlets fail. Besides lower risk, franchises offer the potential for high earnings. People with little knowledge of business can buy into a good company and take advantage of established products and successful business practices.

There are franchises in many different industries: car rental agencies, cleaning services, exercise studios, and so on. All of them function through the sale of licenses, though the fees vary from 1.5 percent to 12 percent of gross sales.

Franchising is becoming more common in many countries because it suits decentralized, service-oriented economies.

1. What is the business relationship between KFC and its franchisees?
2. What are the benefits and risks of franchise ownership? Are there particular advantages for such entrepreneurs as young people, women, or foreigners?
3. Why might franchising be an effective way for a company to expand internationally?
4. What kinds of goods and services are sold through franchises? Can you identify any other goods or services that might be successfully franchised in your area?

5. Strategies for Negotiation: Interrupting to Ask a Question or Make a Comment

During negotiations and meetings of all kinds, it is often necessary—and perfectly acceptable—to interrupt a speaker in order to ask a question or make a comment. Sometimes you may need to ask for clarification or information. At other times, you may want to make a comment to support or expand the point under discussion.

Here are some expressions you can use to interrupt politely to ask a question or to make a comment:

Interrupting to Ask a Question	Interrupting to Make a Comment
Excuse me for interrupting, but...	*If I can just add a point...*
Sorry, may I ask a question?	*Excuse me. I'd like to comment on that.*

1.   Prepare to use the negotiating strategy. Write the expressions in the box on cards or strips of paper. Use the expressions in the exercise below.

2.   Work in pairs. Student A has information. Student B does not. Student A turns to page 152 and reads aloud the information. Student B listens and adds details to the outline below. When either student needs to interrupt to ask a question or make a comment, he or she should use an expression from the cards.

Student B completes this form.

Key Events in KFC History

A. Original KFC Restaurant

    1. Owner _____

    2. Location _____

    3. Menu _____

B. KFC Franchises

    1. Reason for Franchises _____

    2. Number of Franchises _____

C. Sale and Resale of KFC

    1. 1964 Sale _____

    2. 1971 Resale _____

D. Secret KFC Recipe

    1. Protection _____

    2. Location _____

3. Comment on Colonel Sanders as a businessman.

6. Conducting a Business Meeting: Task Forces

A. Preparing for the Meeting

1. Read about the business problem.

> Competition in the fast-food chicken market is intense. Kentucky Fried Chicken is still number one, but competing franchises are growing. The company is anxious to apply the expertise it gained in Japan to other markets. In this meeting, a senior vice president asks task forces, or groups, of KFC international executives to work on solving this problem.
>
> - Where can KFC expand?
> - How can KFC adapt its marketing strategy to new locations?

2. Notice the format of the meeting.

Introduction
- To open the meeting, the senior vice president (SVP) welcomes and introduces everyone.
- The SVP states the purpose of the meeting: to propose new KFC restaurant locations and create marketing strategies adapted to them.

Agenda

- Task forces work independently to come up with ideas for new KFC locations. The SVP moves around the room and listens in on the groups.

- Each task force makes a brief presentation of its proposal to the whole class. When appropriate, participants interrupt to ask questions or make comments.

Closing

- To close the meeting, the SVP thanks all of the executives for their participation. The SVP states that senior management will consider the proposals at an upcoming meeting, and decisions may be made at that time.

3. Review your notes on the KFC-Japan Fact Sheet, the vocabulary, the information on business culture, and the negotiating strategy of the unit. Prepare to use this information in the meeting.

B. Conducting the Meeting

Role play the business meeting.

- Select one person to run the meeting as senior vice president of KFC. Read the role summary below. The SVP will begin the meeting and follow the format described above.

- Form three or four task forces of international KFC executives. Read the role summaries below. Follow the meeting format described.

The Roles

Task Forces of KFC International Executives

Each group of executives decides on a country and city for a new KFC restaurant.
- List opportunities and obstacles for the fast-food market in this country.

- Decide on a marketing strategy adapted to this site. Consider street location, menu adaptations, strategies for on-site and TV advertising, and local traditions that could help the business.

KFC Senior Vice President

You want some good ideas for places to open KFC outlets. You listen in on the task forces, and then begin the meeting when the proposals are ready.

---

7. Follow-Up Activities

A. Business Writing

Write a proposal for a new KFC restaurant location based on your discussion in Exercise 6. Use the information and vocabulary from the unit. Write one paragraph about each of the headings listed. Be sure to use the headings in your proposal.

Proposal for a New KFC Outlet

The Fast Food Market in _____
(select a country)

Opportunities
(Summarize the reasons why the place you have suggested is a good location for a new KFC outlet. You may want to mention, for example, population, wealth, attitudes toward American products, and the popularity of chicken there.)

Obstacles
(Describe one or two possible disadvantages to the suggested location. You may want to consider, for example, local laws and sources of supply.)

A Marketing Strategy for _____
(select a city, country)

Store Location
(Explain the kind of street and building you suggest for the restaurant, and why.)

Menu
(Describe any menu changes or additions to adapt to local taste preferences.)

Advertising
(Describe who the most likely restaurant patrons would be and how to advertise to them. Consider both on-site and TV advertising strategies.)

Local Traditions
(Explain a local tradition that could help increase sales at the new KFC location. For example, you may want to mention how to take advantage of holidays.)

B. Putting the Problem in Perspective: Applying Business Concepts

1. Read the summary below. Comment on the quality of KFC's business decisions.

Adapting to the Japanese Market

The experience of Kentucky Fried Chicken in Japan demonstrates how a company can expand internationally with a carefully adapted marketing approach and a little bit of luck.

At first KFC moved slowly, opening a few test stores. Based on this experience, KFC executives made some key decisions to adapt to the Japanese market. They set up a *joint venture* with Mitsubishi Corporation, with 50 percent of the business owned by each company. This deal *gave* KFC *access* to a ready supply of chicken, since Mitsubishi had *bought into* the chicken and feed business. Another joint venture was set up with a Japanese advertising agency. The creative directors used their knowledge of Japanese eating habits and consumer attitudes to produce TV commercials *capitalizing on* the stylish, U.S. image of KFC. Most of the ads were directed at young housewives and children, the most likely patrons of these fast-food restaurants.

Kentucky Fried Chicken also adapted its menu to *cater to* Japanese tastes. Everyone enjoyed the "finger-lickin' good" chicken, but french fries were substituted for mashed potatoes and a fish selection was added. The company added new outlets quickly, placing them in highly populated areas. To attract and keep quality employees, training was extensive, and ambitious young employees were given management opportunities unusual for people of their age in Japan. Such top managers as Loy Weston's assistant Shin Okuhara made important decisions and helped the business *tune in* to the Japanese way of doing things. Managers were reminded to open their new stores on a lucky day and to bring gifts to local merchants, for example.

Kentucky Fried Chicken's successful entry into Japan was not only the result of *adaptation,* but also some good luck. Kentucky Fried Chicken arrived when the Japanese economy was booming. People had more time and money to eat out. Young people, especially, *were well disposed toward* U.S. social fashions. It also happened that the red and white colors of the store mean happiness in Japan. So successful was KFC's entry into the Japanese market that it was soon followed by such restaurants as McDonald's, Dairy Queen, and Pizza Hut. In a few years, the fast-food industry in Japan had grown by a factor of six.

2. Answer the questions based on what you have learned. Use the italicized expressions in your answers.

a. Why was the *joint venture* with Mitsubishi important to KFC in the beginning? What did Mitsubishi, which had *bought into* some large chicken farms, hope to gain from the deal?

b. The *joint venture* with the Japanese ad agency helped KFC, too. What information did it *give* the company *access to?* How did the ads *capitalize on* this information?

c. How did KFC try to *cater to* the Japanese taste in food, fashion, and culture? Which segments of the population might not *have been* as *well disposed toward* U.S. products as the young people? How could KFC ads and products *cater to* them?

d. Do you think that KFC's success was mostly a question of good timing or of *adaptation*? How important were KFC's efforts to *tune in* to the Japanese style of doing business?

JOHNSON & JOHNSON CONSUMER PRODUCTS, INC.

Making Ethical Decisions in Business

BACKGROUND

1. Examining the Products

Read the information and look at the photograph in order to become familiar with Johnson & Johnson (J&J) and some of its products. Then answer the questions.

Johnson & Johnson Consumer Products, Inc.

- Has its headquarters at One Johnson & Johnson Plaza
  New Brunswick, New Jersey 08933.
- Was founded in 1885.
- Has annual earnings of $618 million.
- Employs 80,000 people.
- Is an international enterprise, with 170 affiliated companies in fifty-five countries.

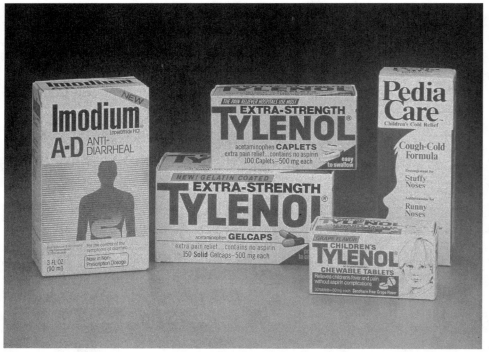

These are some of the many consumer products made by Johnson & Johnson and its related companies. Tylenol, a mild analgesic, or pain reliever, is the company's most profitable single brand. It accounts for over 15 percent of earnings. Tylenol is manufactured by a J&J subsidiary, McNeil Consumer Products Company.

---

1. What are these J&J products generally used for?
2. In the United States, Tylenol and other mild pain relievers are sold in pharmacies and other stores over-the-counter, that is, without a doctor's prescription. Is this a safe practice? Is such medicine sold over-the-counter in other countries?

2. Gathering Data: Listening

You will hear the president of Johnson & Johnson, David Clare, talk with a radio journalist about a tragic event: Seven people in the Chicago area died when they took Extra-Strength Tylenol, a common pain-relieving medicine made by Johnson & Johnson. Someone had opened the capsules and poisoned them with cyanide. Mr. Clare discusses the shocking incident and how people at his company responded to it.

A.   Read the questions. Then listen to the tape and write your answers. Compare your responses with those of a classmate. If you disagree, listen again.

1. According to David Clare, what was the first reaction of people at Johnson & Johnson when they heard the news of the poisonings?
_____
_____

2. In its credo, Johnson & Johnson states its responsibility to its customers and employees. What is that responsibility?
_____
_____

3. The poisoning of Tylenol capsules created an ethical dilemma for J&J executives: If they recalled all of the bottles of Tylenol on the market, what was the danger? If they did not recall Tylenol, what was the danger?
_____
_____

4. What did Johnson & Johnson finally decide to do in response to the poisonings? Why?
_____
_____

5. According to the president of Johnson & Johnson, how did the action of the company probably save some lives?
_____
_____

6. How did the recall of Tylenol help J&J's business?
_____
_____

B.   Discuss your reaction to the interview with David Clare. Did he say anything that interested you particularly? How would you describe his response to the situation? Is this the response you would expect?

3. Gathering Data: Reading

The fact that consumers died from taking poisoned Tylenol, a J&J pain reliever, shocked people all over the world. As a result of the seven deaths in Chicago, Illinois, there were significant changes in the U.S. pharmaceutical industry and in government regulation of that industry.

Read these articles to gather background data on the changes, including information to answer these questions:

• How was drug packaging changed as a result of the Tylenol deaths?
• How did J&J's response to the poisonings affect sales of Tylenol?
• Was the criminal ever identified?

A. Scanning for Information

Work in groups of three. Look at the Tylenol Fact Sheet on page 19. Each person should scan one of the three articles and take notes in the appropriate section of the outline. Then, share information so that everyone in your group has the same data and can fill in the Tylenol Fact Sheet completely.

1. NEW DRUG PACKAGING

The day after Johnson & Johnson's McNeil Consumer Products division learned that some of its popular Tylenol capsules had been poisoned, the company started withdrawing 31 million bottles of Tylenol from store shelves around the country. They were afraid that other bottles might have been tampered with.[1]

At the same time, the company began redesigning the package to restore public confidence. "We called our suppliers and began planning immediately," said William Larsen, McNeil's director of materials management.

Within twenty-four hours, Johnson & Johnson had contacted many of the companies that would be involved in the redesign. By the end of the first week, Johnson & Johnson had decided that the new Tylenol bottle would have three barriers to prevent tampering: a glued box, a "shrink" neckband and an inner seal. (See photo.)

To get Tylenol back on the market, Johnson & Johnson spent $1 million on engravers to redesign 650 pieces of artwork for the product. Cartons and sealing equipment cost more than $5 million during the first few weeks.

By the fifth week after the Chicago deaths, the first 500,000 units of the new tamper-resistant Tylenol package were produced....

While Johnson & Johnson led industry efforts to protect consumers, the Food and Drug Administration, the U.S. government agency that approves products for sale to the public, began developing stronger packaging regulations. As a result, all

Triple safety-sealed, tamper-resistant package for Tylenol capsules has (1) glued flaps on the outer box, (2) a tight plastic neck seal, and (3) a strong inner foil seal over the mouth of the bottle. A bright yellow label on the bottle is imprinted with red letters warning, "Do not use if safety seals are broken."

capsules and liquid drugs must come in tamper-resistant packages. These guidelines also apply to any drugs that are imported into the United States.

1. opened and changed in a harmful way

Tylenol Fact Sheet

1. New Drug Packaging

A. Tamper-Resistant Tylenol

   1. Package design

Three barriers
- *a glued box*
- *a shrink neckband*
- *an inner seal*

   2. Package cost

   3. Production time

B. U.S. Food and Drug Administration Regulations

   1. Domestic drugs

   2. Imported drugs

2. Tylenol's Comeback

A. Chairman Burke's Decision

   1. Recall of Tylenol

Recalled 32 million bottles from stores in U.S.

   2. Opposition to recall

B. Results of the Recall Decision

   1. Tylenol market share

   2. Company attitude

3. The Search for the Criminal

A. Progress of the Search

   1. Tips and reports

Illinois task force
- *checked 60,000 tips*
- *compiled 25,000 pages of reports*
- *conceded the trail is "stone cold"*

   2. Extortion attempt

   3. J&J reward

B. Police Point of View

   1. Doubt

   2. Lack of information

2. TYLENOL'S COMEBACK

After seven innocent people died from taking contaminated Tylenol, sales of the painkiller fell dramatically. But Johnson & Johnson responded to the frightening incident in a notable way. Its executives' decisions turned out to be not only ethical but profitable, too.

James Burke made a decision that will probably be studied in business schools for a long time to come. Going against the advice of government agents and some of his own colleagues, the chairman of Johnson & Johnson decided to spend whatever millions it would cost to recall 31 million bottles of Tylenol capsules from store shelves across the United States. Officials at the <u>Food and Drug Administration</u>[1] feared that the recall would increase the panic already <u>touched off</u>[2] by the poisoning deaths of seven Chicago-area residents who had taken capsules that had been laced with cyanide. The <u>FBI</u>[3] argued that such an expensive action would demonstrate to potential terrorists that they could <u>bring</u> a $5.9 billion corporation <u>to its knees</u>.[4] But Burke prevailed, and his move proved to be decisive in a remarkable and unparalleled winback of public confidence in his company's product.... Tylenol regained more than 80 percent of the market share it held before the still unsolved poisonings.

After the deaths the nonaspirin drug's share of the $1.2 billion painkiller market fell from 35 percent to 7 percent. In a poll, a majority of Tylenol users said they probably would never return to the capsules.

Against such odds, though, Johnson & Johnson and its McNeil Consumer Products subsidiary, the manufacturer of Tylenol, seemed to do everything right. Instead of becoming defensive about the deaths, the company <u>opened its doors and its checkbook</u>.[5] The company fully dedicated itself to the investigation, says Tyrone Fahner, who headed the probe during his term as Illinois attorney general. Said he: "Anything we wanted from them, we got. The president of the company called and asked if I thought a reward might help. Before I could raise the possibility of $20,000, he was asking if $100,000 would be enough."

1. U.S. government agency that approves food and drug products for sale to the public
2. suddenly started
3. Federal Bureau of Investigation: the central U.S. government police agency
4. ruin
5. willingly spoke to the media and spent money to help solve the problem

3. THE SEARCH FOR THE CRIMINAL

People all over the world were horrified by the deaths of seven innocent people who took Tylenol capsules laced with deadly cyanide. It seemed that anyone could have bought those deadly pills, and anyone could have died from ingesting them. This element of randomness was particularly frightening.

There was a huge effort by the city of Chicago, the state of Illinois, and the entire United States to find the criminal. However, the search for the Tylenol killer has not been successful.

The Illinois task force, reduced to ten agents from 150, has checked out 60,000 tips and compiled 25,000 pages of reports. Though the investigators work relentlessly, one of them concedes that the trail is "stone cold,[1] and has been for six months." James W. Lewis, who is accused of trying to extort[2] $1 million from Johnson & Johnson by offering to "stop the killing," will go on trial. Police have failed to find evidence connecting Lewis directly with the poisonings.

Johnson & Johnson's $100,000 reward still stands,[3] but Illinois agents doubt that anyone will ever collect it. Says Thomas Schumpp of the Illinois department of law enforcement: "With Tylenol there was never a message or a clue to the reason. Not only can't we say who, but we can't say why."

1. there are no more helpful clues to investigate
2. obtain by threat
3. is offered

B. Interpreting Information

Review the information on your Tylenol Fact Sheet. Read each statement below. Decide whether you agree or disagree with it. Write *agree* or *disagree* in the blank. Work in small groups. Compare your answers with those of your classmates, and explain your opinions. There is no one right answer.

_____ 1. The redesigned Tylenol package is as tamper-resistant as possible.

_____ 2. The FDA packaging guidelines have probably caused drug manufacturers in other countries to make their packaging more tamper-resistant.

_____ 3. If the chairman of the board of Johnson & Johnson had not recalled Tylenol, the U.S. government would have done it.

_____ 4. Johnson & Johnson withdrew Tylenol in order to avoid lawsuits from other consumers who might be hurt by the product.

_____ 5. If Johnson & Johnson had given more money to the search, the criminal would have been found.

_____ 6. If Johnson & Johnson were not so large and wealthy, the company would have been ruined by the poisonings.

C. Reviewing Background Information and Vocabulary

Read the sentences and find the word or expression in the box that means the same as the italicized words. Then compare your answers with those of a classmate. If you disagree, consult another classmate, a dictionary, or your teacher.

a. was in the end

b. investigated

c. very difficult choice

d. very common

e. because of the slight possibility

f. suddenly started

g. honesty

h. care a great deal about

i. medicines

j. without a doctor's prescription

_____ 1. Johnson & Johnson is a *household* name in baby-care as well as medical products. Nearly every family in the United States has in its house at least one product made by this company.

_____ 2. Johnson & Johnson enjoys a reputation for high-quality products and business *integrity*. Consumers feel that they can trust J&J products.

_____ 3. Trust is a big issue for a firm that makes *pharmaceuticals*. Customers must believe that the products improve, not endanger, their health.

_____ 4. According to its credo, the J&J company is required to *place a high priority on* the needs of customers. Protecting customers is the company's first concern.

_____ 5. The Tylenol case was particularly frightening because it involved drugs available *over-the-counter* that any person could have purchased and used.

_____ 6. The Tylenol poisonings posed a *dilemma* for Johnson & Johnson. There would be negative results whether the company recalled the product or did not recall it.

_____ 7. The company decided to recall Tylenol *on the off chance* that other contaminated bottles were on store shelves. It was impossible to know if other bottles had been poisoned.

_____ 8. The recall *turned out to be* good for business. Tylenol not only regained but increased its share of the market.

_____ 9. The Tylenol poisonings *touched off* a revolution in drug packaging in the United States. Almost every package had to be redesigned to meet new standards.

_____ 10. Although the police said that they *checked out* all possible clues in this case, the criminal has never been identified.

PART 2

MAKING DECISIONS—MAKING ETHICAL DECISIONS IN BUSINESS

Introduction to the Problem. After J&J's Tylenol product was contaminated with deadly cyanide, the company invested millions in recalling Tylenol and creating new tamper-resistant packaging. Four years after the first incident, another person died after taking poisoned Tylenol from a so-called tamper-resistant package. Johnson & Johnson is faced again with the problem of winning back the public trust. To do this, it must get the media on its side.

Keep the problem in mind as you do the following exercises.

4. Exploring Business Culture: Business Ethics

Read each statement about a business practice related to ethics at Johnson & Johnson. Then, check [✔] whether you consider them usual or unusual business practices. In small groups, compare your answers and discuss the ones you have checkmarked as unusual.

Aspects of Business Ethics at Johnson & Johnson

	Usual	Unusual
1. The ethics of business decisions are discussed openly and frequently.		
2. There is a written code of ethics, or credo.		
3. The code of ethics is communicated to customers, stockholders, and the media.		
4. In a crisis, executives of the company talk directly to news reporters.		
5. In a crisis, top executives take responsibility by staying in their positions, rather than by resigning.		
6. Company executives, not government officials, decide when a product that has had a problem can be returned to the market.		

5. Strategies for Negotiation: Answering Difficult Questions

As a business executive, you may have to work with a public relations department in your company or face news reporters yourself, especially if your business has a crisis. Your performance in these situations can enhance your image and that of your company, or it can cause serious damage. Knowing how to answer difficult or even hostile questions can help you a great deal.

Here are two techniques, and appropriate expressions, to help you answer difficult questions.

Technique 1: *Paraphrase Questions.* By putting difficult questions in your own words, you take control of them and give yourself a moment to think.

In other words, you're asking…

So, what you want to know is…

Technique 2: *Repeat your message.* Answer the question you are asked. But look at the question as an opportunity to bridge to the main message *you* would like to communicate.

And that brings us to the main issue here.

So, you can see that the point is…

1. Prepare to use the negotiating strategy. Write the techniques and expressions for answering difficult questions on cards or strips of paper. Use these techniques and expressions in the exercise below.

2. Work in small groups. Discuss one or more of these situations. Some students will ask questions; others will answer. When you answer a difficult question, use a technique and an expression from your cards.

a. After the first poisonings, several J&J executives are interviewed by FBI agents. The agents ask difficult questions about who may have tampered with the capsules and how the tampering was possible. The J&J executives insist that their factories are completely secure.

b. Reporters from a news program want to find out from FBI and Illinois state officials why the criminal has not been caught yet. The reporters ask hostile questions about the quality of the investigation. The law enforcement officials emphasize that they are doing everything possible to find the killer.

6. Conducting a Business Meeting: A News Conference

A. Preparing for the Meeting

1. Read about the business problem.

It is now four years after the first poisonings. Unbelievably, another woman has just died from taking Tylenol laced with cyanide, twenty-three-year-old Diane Elsroth of Peekskill, New York. Today, shocked J&J executives have called a news conference to tell their story to the public through the media.

- What can Johnson & Johnson do to win back public confidence in its products this time?

- If tamper-resistant packaging does not work, how can Johnson & Johnson protect the consumer?

- What can Johnson & Johnson do to find the criminal?

---

2. Notice the format of the meeting.

Introduction
- James Burke, chairman of the board of Johnson & Johnson, opens the news conference by welcoming everyone and thanking them for coming.
- Mr. Burke states the purpose of the news conference: to let everyone know that Johnson & Johnson is doing everything possible to protect consumers and find the criminal.

Agenda
- Each group meets to discuss the problem from its point of view. Burke moves around the room and listens in on the groups.
- Burke invites the news reporters to ask questions of him or any member of the J&J Crisis Team. When the news reporters ask difficult questions, the executives use appropriate techniques and expressions to answer them.

Closing
- Burke closes the news conference with a statement in which he repeats his main message: Johnson & Johnson is so concerned about safety that it is redesigning all capsules and actively participating in all aspects of the investigation.

3. Review your notes on the Tylenol Fact Sheet, the vocabulary, the information on business culture, and the negotiating strategy in the unit. Prepare to use this information in the news conference.

B. Conducting the Meeting

Role play the news conference.

- Select one person to run the news conference as James Burke. Mr. Burke will begin the meeting and follow the format described above.
- Form one group of news reporters and one group of J&J executives. Read the role summaries below and on p. 27. Follow the format described.

The Roles

J&J Crisis Management Team

You are anxious to reassure the public that Johnson & Johnson will uphold its credo and do everything possible to protect the safety of its customers. You want to emphasize that:

- Johnson & Johnson is cooperating fully with federal and local investigators to solve the crime.
- Our credo will guide our actions: All Tylenol capsules will be recalled and replaced with caplets, solid pills that are easier to swallow and cannot be opened.
- J&J quality control prevents any tampering at the factory.
- *(Add your own.)*

This drawing illustrates the essential difference between capsules and caplets. Capsules have two parts that slip into one another. They can be opened. In contrast, caplets are solid pills that cannot be opened.

News Reporters

For a national newspaper, you want to know:

- How the poisoned capsules got into the victim's hands.
- Whether the criminal might be an unhappy J&J employee.
- If FDA regulations for drug packaging are strict enough.
- *(Add your own.)*

For a a story in the local newspaper serving the victim's community, you want to know:

- How Johnson & Johnson plans to compensate the victim's family.
- Where the poisoned Tylenol was purchased.
- What consumers should do with Tylenol they have at home.
- *(Add your own.)*

For a story in a financial newspaper, you want to know:

- If Johnson & Johnson will stop making Tylenol since its stock price has fallen drastically.
- If packaging will again be redesigned, making packagers' stock prices soar.
- Whether competitors will also replace capsules with solid pills (caplets).
- *(Add your own.)*

7. Follow-Up Activities

A. Business Writing

1. Read the business letter. Notice its form and content. Work in pairs. Read the questions on the left. Discuss your answers.

1. Most business letters in English follow a similar format. Notice the introductory information.

   a. Business stationery, or letterhead, has a preprinted address. If you use plain paper, where does your address appear?

   b. The date is usually placed on the right-hand side. What other information appears on the right-hand side of a letter?

   c. What is included in the receiver's address?

   d. The most common greeting for business as well as personal letters is *dear*. Have you seen any others?

2. The body of the letter usually has three short paragraphs.

   a. The first paragraph establishes a relationship between the receiver and the sender. What is the relationship here?

   b. The second paragraph briefly states the purpose of the letter. What is the purpose here?

   c. The final paragraph clearly indicates the action that is expected. What does this sender expect?

3. Notice the standard closing information in a business letter.

   a. *Sincerely* is the most common closing. Have you seen others?

   b. The sender's signature appears above his or her printed name. Why?

   c. The sender alerts the receiver to any copies of the letter sent to others. How? Why? If the sender has enclosed something with the letter, the word "Enclosure" (or "Enc") appears here. Why?

2031 Oak Drive
Westport, CT 06880
March 30, 19___

Mr. James Burke
Chairman of the Board
Johnson & Johnson
1 Johnson & Johnson Plaza
New Brunswick, NJ 08933

Dear Mr. Burke:

As a J&J stockholder, I am very distressed about the future of Tylenol now that the product has been tampered with a second time.

Despite your assurances to the public through the media, I am not convinced that caplets will eliminate tampering. In my view, the packaging must be improved, factory security must be tightened, and Johnson & Johnson must tell the public more about its efforts to catch the criminals. Otherwise, the investors will continue to suffer from declining stock prices.

These concerns of J&J stockholders must be addressed immediately. I look forward to hearing your plans.

Sincerely,

Jean M. Boyle
Jean M. Boyle

cc Mr. David Clare, president of J&J

---

2. Business letters in English are usually simple, clear, and short. They are written from the point of view of the reader. Compare the sample business letter in English to business letters in your language. Consider style, content, and purpose.

3. Write a business letter. As James Burke, chairman of the board of Johnson & Johnson, explain to your stockholders what has happened, how J&J is responding to the crisis, and what J&J's business prospects are for the coming year. Begin your letter, "Dear Stockholders:"

Making Ethical Decisions in Business

B. Putting the Problem in Perspective: Applying Business Concepts

1. Read the selection below. Comment on the quality of J&J's business decisions.

To some people, the concept of *business ethics* may be a contradiction. In other words, they may view business managers as responsible only for making profits, not for upholding standards of integrity. But in two major company crises, the international pharmaceutical company Johnson & Johnson found that placing a high priority on ethics can turn out to be good for business.

Tylenol is a *leading* over-the-counter analgesic produced by a subsidiary of Johnson & Johnson. When people who took Tylenol to relieve pain ended up dying from the product, J&J executives were faced with a dilemma: Should they spend millions to *recall* the product and perhaps encourage similar crimes, or should they simply replace the product in people's homes and hope that no other bottles of Tylenol were contaminated? The answer came from the company's *credo*. J&J President David Clare stated: "First and foremost, we had to protect the public." To do this, the company withdrew millions of bottles and replaced millions more without cost to the customer, on the off chance that other bottles might be poisoned.

After the first crisis, the U.S. Federal Drug Administration imposed new *regulations* to make drug packaging *tamper-resistant*. No packaging, however, can be tamperproof, which was sadly proven by the second crisis. Another person died from swallowing Tylenol capsules laced with cyanide. At this point, J&J executives were again guided by their company credo. They imposed their own higher standard, and changed from making capsules to caplets, in order to provide a safer product.

Both crises touched off a debate on business ethics and integrity. Yet, after each one, J&J executives managed to restore public confidence and Tylenol *made a comeback*. J&J showed the public that it cared about the consumer, and the product increased its market share.

2. Answer the questions based on what you have learned. Use the italicized expressions in your answers.

a. Do you think it is necessary or even possible for every company to have clearly stated *business ethics*? Do some companies, such as pharmaceutical firms, need a *credo* more than others?

b. When a *leading* consumer product is found to be unsafe, what is the responsibility of the manufacturer: Must the company *recall* the product, warn people to get rid of the product, or pay compensation for injury? Should the government take action?

c. After the Tylenol crises, drug packaging in the United States was made *tamper-resistant*. Which groups of people benefited from the new government *regulations*? Who pays for the packaging? Should all packaging for over-the-counter drugs sold everywhere be tamper-resistant?

d. Many people thought that the deaths would destroy Tylenol as a brand name, but the product *made a comeback* twice. does this surprise you? Can you give examples of other products than were (or were not) able to *make a comeback* after a serious safety crisis?

C. The Johnson & Johnson Credo

Read the document, then discuss your answers to the questions.

Our Credo

We believe our first responsibility is to the doctors, nurses and patients,
to mothers and fathers and all others who use our products and services.
In meeting their needs everything we do must be of high quality.
We must constantly strive to reduce our costs
in order to maintain reasonable prices.
Customers' orders must be serviced promptly and accurately.
Our suppliers and distributors must have an opportunity
to make a fair profit.

We are responsible to our employees,
the men and women who work with us throughout the world.
Everyone must be considered as an individual.
We must respect their dignity and recognize their merit.
They must have a sense of security in their jobs.
Compensation must be fair and adequate,
and working conditions clean, orderly and safe.
We must be mindful of ways to help our employees fulfill
their family responsibilities.
Employees must feel free to make suggestions and complaints.
There must be equal opportunity for employment, development
and advancement for those qualified.
We must provide competent management,
and their actions must be just and ethical.

We are responsible to the communities in which we live and work
and to the world community as well.
We must be good citizens — support good works and charities
and bear our fair share of taxes.
We must encourage civic improvements and better health and education.
We must maintain in good order
the property we are privileged to use,
protecting the environment and natural resources.

Our final responsibility is to our stockholders.
Business must make a sound profit.
We must experiment with new ideas.
Research must be carried on, innovative programs developed
and mistakes paid for.
New equipment must be purchased, new facilities provided
and new products launched.
Reserves must be created to provide for adverse times.
When we operate according to these principles,
the stockholders should realize a fair return.

Johnson & Johnson

1. What is your opinion of this document? Does anything in it surprise you?
2. Do you think most business people agree that their first responsibility is to their customers and their last responsibility is to their stockholders?

BEN & JERRY'S HOMEMADE, INC.

Developing a Compensation Policy

BACKGROUND

1. Examining the Products

Read the information and look at the photographs in order to become familiar with Ben & Jerry's Homemade and some of its products. Then answer the questions.

Ben & Jerry's Homemade, Inc.

- Is located at Route 100, P.O. Box 240
  Waterbury, Vermont 05676.
- Was founded in 1978.
- Has annual earnings of $50 million.
- Employs 350 people.

This is the carton for Rainforest Crunch—vanilla ice cream with buttercrunch candy made with Brazil nuts and cashews grown in the rain forest.

These are a few of Ben & Jerry's more than thirty ice cream flavors:

Cherry Garcia: French vanilla ice cream with big cherries and chunks of dark chocolate

Chocolate Fudge Brownie: chocolate ice cream with chunks of dense chocolate cakelike cookie

Chunky Monkey: banana ice cream made from fresh bananas, walnuts, and chunks of chocolate

Heath Bar Crunch: vanilla ice cream with chunks of butter candy

New York Super Fudge Chunk: chocolate ice cream with pecans, walnuts, almonds, and chunks of white and dark chocolate

Strawberry: strawberry ice cream with fresh strawberries and a hint of lemon

---

1. What does Ben & Jerry's Homemade want you to think about its products? Consider product name and packaging.
2. Ben & Jerry's ice cream is a superpremium, or rich and expensive, brand. The company produces many Euphoric Flavors to make its customers happy. Which of Ben & Jerry's ice cream flavors would you like to try? Compare these flavors with the ice cream flavors you already know.
3. What are some of the differences between high-quality and low-quality ice cream?

2. Gathering Data: Listening

You will hear a tape about Ben Cohen and Jerry Greenfield, two old friends who decided to go into the ice cream business together. "Caring capitalism," which describes Ben and Jerry's unusual and highly successful approach to business, is discussed on the tape.

A.   Read the questions. Then listen to the tape and write your answers. Compare your responses with those of a classmate. If you disagree, listen again.

1. Ben and Jerry learned how to make ice cream by taking a course and by experimenting with new recipes. What are some of the characteristics of the ice cream they created?

   _____

   _____

2. At first, the ice cream was sold only at Ben & Jerry's Ice Cream Shop in Burlington, Vermont. Soon after, it became available in many types of places. Can you list three types?

   _____

   _____

3. To finance a new ice cream plant, Ben & Jerry's Homemade sold stock (ownership) in the company. Why did the company offer the stock to people in Vermont?

   _____

   _____

4. Ben & Jerry's Homemade has a three-part mission statement. Can you give an example related to each part of the mission?

   a. social responsibility

   _____

   b. product quality

   _____

   c. economic responsibility

   _____

5. Ben & Jerry believe in the concept of "caring capitalism." What is the main idea of this approach to business?

   _____

   _____

B.   Discuss your reaction to the tape about Ben and Jerry. Did anything about them surprise or interest you particularly? What do you think of their way of doing business?

3. Gathering Data: Reading

Ben & Jerry's Homemade is well known for superpremium ice cream and "caring capitalism," a socially responsible approach to business. Its founders believe that business must be actively involved in local and global issues.

Read these articles to gather background data on the company, including information to answer these questions:

- What is Ben & Jerry's Homemade doing to help dairy farmers in Vermont?
- How is this Vermont ice cream company trying to help save the rain forest of Brazil?
- What is Ben & Jerry's Homemade doing to promote international peace?

A. Scanning for Information

Work in groups of three. Look at the outline of Ben & Jerry's Projects on page 35. Each person should scan one of the three articles and take notes in the appropriate section of the outline. Then, share the information so that everyone in your group has the same data and can fill in the outline of Ben & Jerry's Projects completely.

1. FARM PROJECT

Ben & Jerry's Homemade is located in Vermont, a northeastern state of the United States whose local economy relies heavily on dairy products. The company believes that Vermont's small family farms are threatened by a new drug, bovine growth hormone, or BGH. When injected into dairy cattle, BGH can increase milk production significantly. According to Ben & Jerry's, the only beneficiaries of the commercial use of BGH will be the four large chemical companies who have developed the drug.

Ben & Jerry's Homemade points out that the drug poses important economic and safety problems. If approved by the government, BGH will increase milk production, drive down milk prices and soon force the small family farmer out of business. As a result, community life in Vermont and other rural areas will be disrupted and the land will fall into the hands of unsympathetic owners. Moreover, too little is known about the effects of BGH on humans. As concern for the <u>wholesomeness</u>[1] of the food supply rises, BGH will create confusion about dairy products, further eroding the state's economy and well-being.

To fight the approval of BGH, Ben & Jerry's is educating the public. It urges people to read about the issue and to write to their elected officials. At the same time, the company makes sure that its own products <u>are free from</u>[2] BGH. Ben & Jerry's supports Vermont farms by purchasing all of its milk and cream from a cooperative owned and operated by 500 local family farmers. Ben & Jerry's believes that these farmers are important to the heritage and quality of life in Vermont and throughout the United States.

1. healthfulness
2. do not have

2. RAIN FOREST PROJECT

Ben & Jerry's is very involved in projects to protect the environment. Company executives believe that business can make a profit without destroying the earth.

If the <u>profit motive</u>[1] has helped destroy the Amazonian rain forests, can it be used to save them? Estimates say that Brazil's ranchers, loggers, and farmers have already <u>eradicated</u>[2] as much as 12 percent of the world's largest rain forest. Now environmentalists are counting on capitalism to <u>lure a new breed</u>[3] of treasure hunter. Rather than destroying the land for riches, . . . entrepreneurs are seeking native herbs for cosmetics, exotic fish for food . . . and untold other products that won't harm the land. "We want to show that a living rain forest makes more money than a dead rain forest," says Jason Clay, research director of the Harvard University–affiliated organization Cultural Survival.

Businessmen are wasting no time <u>cashing in</u>.[4] Ben & Jerry's Homemade Ice Cream recently introduced a flavor featuring Brazil nuts and cashews called Rainforest Crunch. . . . The company will donate a portion of the profits to rain forest conservation efforts. Clay argues that nut farming not only conserves the forest but is five times as profitable per acre as cattle ranching—and nut farmers do not have to spend money putting up fences, clearing land or hiring cowboys.

1. desire to gain money
2. completely destroyed
3. attract a new kind
4. making money

Ben and Jerry's Projects

1. Farm Project	**2. Rain Forest Project**	**3. Peace Project**
A. Dairy Farm Issue	A. Rain Forest Issue	A. Ben & Jerry's Product
1. Drug for dairy cattle	1. Old entrepreneurs	1. Peace Pop ice cream
2. Problems with the drug	2. New entrepreneurs	2. Peace Pop goal
B. Ben & Jerry's Activities	B. Ben & Jerry's Activities	B. 1% for Peace Program
1. Public education	1. New product	1. Ben & Jerry's donations
2. Purchase of ingredients	2. Financial contributions and environmental benefits	2. Program activities

3. PEACE PROJECT

Ben & Jerry's puts some of its profits into such global projects as a not-for-profit organization to promote peace through research and education. A percentage of profits from sales of one of its products, the Peace Pop, are given to this project. A Peace Pop is ice cream on a stick, covered in thick chocolate....

Ben & Jerry's, the Vermont-based ice cream maker, is encouraging Americans to pig out[1] for peace. The company is promoting a Peace Pop, a confection with weighty[2] goals: Its box states that "peace throughout the world is a possible dream that can be achieved in our lifetime."...

Ben and Jerry promise to give 1 percent of their pretax profits to a program they helped found, 1% for Peace. The group, based in Ithaca, N.Y., advocates that 1 percent of the nation's defense budget go to peace-mongering[3] activities such as the Rocky Mountain Institute Project (a summer-camp exchange between U.S. and Soviet teens) and the Center for Innovative Diplomacy, which gets local governments to kibitz[4] on foreign policy.... With only one cent of every dollar going to the effort, cynics might say products like Peace Pop use pacifism as a marketing ploy.[5] Company co-founder Ben Cohen shrugs off the gibes[6]: "Maybe we should show that peace is profitable."

1. eat too much
2. This is a play on words, meaning *serious* as well as *high-calorie and fattening*
3. peace-seeking
4. talk together informally
5. trick to gain an advantage
6. insulting comments

This is the package of Ben & Jerry's Peace Pop. When you buy this product, you enjoy quality ice cream and contribute to an organization that promotes peace.

B. Interpreting Information

Review the information in your Ben & Jerry's Project outline. Read each statement below. Decide whether you agree or disagree with it. Write *agree* or *disagree* in the blank. Work in small groups. Compare your answers with those of your classmates, and explain your opinions. There is no one right answer.

_____ 1. The Farm Project has a better chance of succeeding than the Rain Forest Project because it is a local effort.

_____ 2. The most interesting project is the one involving Peace Pops because it has the most potential influence worldwide.

_____ 3. Ben & Jerry's should use more of its profits to benefit its local employees and community rather than to support global projects.

_____ 4. These Ben & Jerry's projects are nothing more than good advertising.

_____ 5. If the company were not growing fast and making a huge profit, it would not undertake any of these projects.

C. Reviewing Background Information and Vocabulary

Read the sentences and find the word or expression in the box that means the same as the italicized words. Then compare your answers with those of a classmate. If you disagree, consult another classmate, a dictionary, or your teacher.

a. great happiness

b. pieces

c. strongly recommend

d. lower

e. rich and expensive

f. ate too much

g. healthful

h. into bankruptcy

i. serious

j. gives

k. sales

_____ 1. Ben & Jerry's Homemade is a *superpremium* brand. Its high butterfat and low air content make it heavy and creamy. Unlike most ice creams available in supermarkets, it is sold in pint (0.473 liter) cartons.

_____ 2. The company emphasizes that its products are *wholesome* because they are made with fresh Vermont cream, eggs, fruit, and other natural ingredients.

_____ 3. Ben & Jerry's Homemade ice cream comes in distinctive flavors. The company founders have always had fun creating flavors capable of putting people in a state of *euphoria*.

_____ 4. "Last night we ate an entire carton of Rainforest Crunch, the flavor with nuts from Brazil. This ice cream is so good that we just *pigged out*."

_____ 5. Ben & Jerry's Homemade is known for mixing candy, cookies, and nuts into ice cream. New York Superfudge Chunk, for example, contains large *chunks* of white and dark chocolate, as well as almonds, pecans, and walnuts.

_____ 6. To Ben Cohen and Jerry Greenfield, business can be a powerful force for positive change in society. They involve their company in such *weighty* issues as global peace and environmental protection.

_____ 7. Ben & Jerry *advocate* using the rain forest in a productive and careful way, not just saving it. They have a nut-shelling project in Brazil to demonstrate their idea.

_____ 8. The company *donates* some of its profits to research and educational organizations that work on such issues as reducing the U.S. budget for defense.

_____ 9. Ben & Jerry's Homemade started very small. Soon *demand* increased so much that they had to build a new factory to expand ice cream production.

_____10. Increased competition in the market could *drive down* Ben & Jerry's profits in the future. The company has several competitors now.

_____11. A few years ago, a large company tried to force Ben & Jerry's Homemade *out of business* by controlling the ice cream distributing companies. Ben & Jerry's showed that this practice was illegal.

MAKING DECISIONS—DEVELOPING A COMPENSATION POLICY

Introduction to the Problem. Caring capitalism is central to Ben & Jerry's way of doing business. It means undertaking social and environmental projects outside the company. It also means treating the company's own employees with unusual respect. One of Ben & Jerry's major problems is deciding how much money employees should earn.

Keep the problem in mind as you do the following exercises.

4. Exploring Business Culture: Employer-Employee Relations

Read each statement about a business practice related to employer-employee relations at Ben & Jerry's. Then, check [✔] whether you consider them usual or unusual business practices. In small groups, compare your answers and discuss the ones you have checkmarked as unusual.

Aspects of Employer-Employee Relations at Ben & Jerry's

	Usual	Unusual
1. Employees have many opportunities to speak with and write to the highest executives in the company.		
2. Employees are encouraged to express their concerns openly at meetings.		
3. The opinions of employees have a significant influence on the policies made by top executives.		
4. Employees of all ranks meet together several times a year to discuss company issues.		
5. Employees know approximately how much everyone else in the company earns.		
6. All employees have stock (ownership) in the company.		

5. Strategies for Negotiation: Conceding a Point

In order to negotiate effectively as a business manager, you need to be able to recognize what is right about what your co-worker, employee, or client says before you disagree with it. If you begin by conceding that the other person has made a good point, that person will be much more likely to pay attention to your view.

Here are some expressions you can use to concede a point:

> *Granted that... However,...*   *You're right about that. Still,...*
> *Admittedly,...*

1. **Prepare to use the negotiating strategy. Write the expressions in the box on cards or strips of paper. Use these expressions in the exercise below.**

2. **Work in small groups. Discuss one or more of these situations. Give your own ideas and opinions. When you want to disagree, first concede a point, then state your disagreement.**

    a. Ben & Jerry's Homemade might try to develop a low-fat ice cream. Is this a good business idea?

    b. Imagine that the University of Vermont, the major public university in the state, has approached Ben & Jerry's for a donation. Should the company contribute? If so, what kind of contribution should it make? Decide on one of the following:

- scholarships for children of farmers

- an extension to the business school building

- support for a new professor's position in environmental studies

6. Conducting a Business Meeting: A Staff Meeting

A. Preparing for the Meeting

1. **Read about the business problem.**

> For several years, Ben & Jerry's Homemade has had a compressed salary ratio: The highest paid employee earns no more than five times what the lowest paid employee earns. Now this policy has become a problem.
>
> - How can the company recruit new managers when the salaries are relatively low?
>
> - Should Ben & Jerry's Homemade change the compensation policy? If so, in what way?

2. Notice the format of the meeting.

Introduction
- Ben Cohen, a founder of the company, opens the meeting by welcoming and introducing everyone.
- Ben states the purpose of the meeting: to discuss whether to maintain or change the current five-to-one compensation policy.

Agenda
- Each group meets to discuss the problem from its point of view. Ben moves around the room and listens in on the groups.
- Ben invites all participants to state their views on the five-to-one compensation policy and to offer alternatives. When appropriate, participants concede points before they disagree.

Closing
- Ben summarizes the main points made during the meeting.
- He closes the meeting by thanking everyone. He asks the board of directors to meet separately to vote on whether to maintain or revise the compensation policy. He invites participants to respond to their decision by writing him an interoffice letter.

3. Review your notes on Ben & Jerry's Projects, the vocabulary, the information on business culture, and the negotiating strategy in the unit. Prepare to use this information in the meeting.

B. Conducting a Meeting

Role play the staff meeting.

- Select one person to run the meeting as Ben, chairman of the board of directors and chief executive officer (CEO). Ben will begin the meeting and follow the format described above.
- Form three groups: the board of directors, the management group, and the nonmanagerial staff. Read the role summaries on page 41. Follow the meeting format described.

The Roles

Board of Directors

You created the five-to-one compensation policy and defend it for many reasons.

- The salary ratio links the success of people at the top with the success of people at the bottom of the company. It is socially responsible.
- Keeping salaries reasonable allows the company to spend 7.5 percent of pretax profits on such socially responsible efforts as the farm, rain forest, and peace projects.
- The compressed ratio helps attract people who share the values of the company.
- The ratio helps recognize the importance of the workers who actually make the product.
- *(Add your own.)*

Management Group

You are divided in your opinion. You all deeply respect the board of directors, and some of you agree with them. Others, however, believe the policy should be changed.

- The company has trouble hiring and retaining good executives because the salaries are low.
- If you help the company earn more, you should get more for yourself.
- Ben & Jerry's executives should be able to earn bonuses or stock options, or participate in profit-sharing to increase their salaries.
- The needs of the company are changing, so the policy must change.
- *(Add your own.)*

Nonmanagerial Staff

You make and package the ice cream, work in the offices, and keep them clean. You believe the five-to-one compensation ratio should not be changed.

- The compressed salary ratio helps provide decent salaries and benefits for community people.
- The company's compensation policy helps people feel proud of their work and of themselves.
- Equitable salaries unify all employees in the enterprise.
- The policy is more suitable and effective than a union organization.
- *(Add your own.)*

7. Follow-Up Activities

1. Interoffice letters differ from other business letters in format.

   a. Where does information about the receiver, sender, and date appear? How does this format differ from that of a business letter?

   b. What information appears next to "Re," meaning "regarding"?

   c. Where does the sender "sign" an interoffice letter?

2. The body of an interoffice letter often has three or four short paragraphs.

   a. The first paragraph contains the main message. What is the message here?

   b. Subsequent paragraphs answer key questions that the reader is likely to have about the message. What is the question answered by the second paragraph?

   c. What question is answered by the third paragraph? Why does the writer list his points?

3. An interoffice letter has no formal closing. What is the purpose of the brief concluding paragraph?

A. Business Writing

1. **Read the interoffice letter, or memo. This kind of letter is written from one person to another within the same company. Work in pairs to answer the questions on the left.**

VERMONT'S FINEST ALL NATURAL ICE CREAM™

Route 100, P.O. Box 240, Waterbury, Vermont 05676 (802) 244-5641; Marketing Office 244-6957

Interoffice Letter

```
To:     Ben Cohen, Chairman of the Board
From:   Chico Lager, Chief Operating Officer  CL
Re:     Compensation Policy Revision
Date:   February 15, _____
```

We need to meet with the management group to discuss our compensation policy.

As you know, we have recently had problems hiring a good chief financial officer because of our salary ratio. You may not know that some of our current executives may leave for better salaries elsewhere.

To make compensation more flexible, I suggest we consider one or more of the following:

- expanding the five-to-one ratio to six- or seven-to-one;
- adding to executive salaries with profit-sharing or stock options;
- raising base salaries with some of the 7.5% set aside for projects;
- creating opportunities for executives to earn bonuses based on performance.

With your approval, I'll call a general meeting of the management group for next Friday at 9:00 A.M.

We Support

2. **Compare this sample interoffice letter to the business letter on page 28. Consider style, content, and purpose.**

3. **Compare the sample interoffice letter in English to interoffice letters in your language. Consider style, content, and purpose.**

4. **Write an interoffice letter to Ben Cohen as a member of the management group or nonmanagerial staff. State whether the five-to-one salary ratio should be changed or not, and why.**

Socially Responsible Business

B. Putting the Problem in Perspective: Applying Business Concepts

1. Read the summary below. Comment on the quality of Ben & Jerry's business decisions.

In ten years, Ben and Jerry turned an $8,000 investment into a $50,000,000 business. Ben & Jerry's is very strong in the superpremium ice cream market, second only to the giant Pillsbury Corporation that makes Haagen-Dazs Ice Cream. Ben, a college drop-out who had a series of low-paying jobs, and his old friend Jerry, a lab technician who could not get into medical school, clearly represent a new breed of *entrepreneur*. As Jerry has said, "We grew up in the sixties, when it wasn't cool to be businessmen." From the start, the slogan of their company has been, "If it isn't fun, why do it?" These unconventional executives have blended wholesome ingredients and an informal attitude to create a new style of doing business, sometimes called a "business counterculture." They have become *prosperous*, but they have been equally concerned about promoting such weighty social issues as peace and the environment.

At home, the business partners demonstrate their philosophy of *caring capitalism* by supporting small family farms, selling their company's stock to Vermonters, and donating money to conservation groups. Abroad, they have cashed in on interest in the environment, creating a nut-shelling operation in Brazil to help save the rain forest. Customers of Ben & Jerry's Homemade who eat ice cream prepared with these nuts feel they are helping to solve the problem.

Within the company, Ben & Jerry's Homemade struggles to maintain a fair *compensation policy*. Though the *profit motive* is essential to business, the company has tried to hire people with an equal concern for community values. As the business has grown, the *compressed salary ratio* policy has become controversial. Instead of throwing it out, though, executives at Ben & Jerry's have decided to expand the ratio.

Ben & Jerry's caring capitalism has inspired others to create businesses that care about employees and give back to the community, notably the very successful British skin and haircare firm called The Body Shop. Meanwhile, demand for what *Time* magazine called "the best ice cream in the world" remains strong.

2. Answer the questions based on what you have learned. Use the italicized words or expressions in your answers.

a. What are some of the reasons for Ben and Jerry's success as *entrepreneurs*? Do you have an idea for a new euphoric flavor? Could their *entrepreneurial* style be effective in other countries?

b. *Caring capitalism* involves a blending of economic and social goals. Do you know of other businesses that operate in a socially responsible way? Would you enjoy working for a company like this?

c. Ben and Jerry believe that the *profit motive* can be linked to people's desire to do good. Do you agree? Can this idea work only in *prosperous* times? If so, does it make the work any less important? What community or global projects would you suggest to Ben & Jerry's Homemade?

d. Why is the *compressed salary ratio* important at Ben & Jerry's? Should a *compensation policy* be based on a ratio? Would you like to work under such a policy?

LEVI STRAUSS & CO.

Applying Market Research to New Product Development

Unit 4

PART 1

BACKGROUND

1. Examining the Products

Read the information and look at the photographs in order to become familiar with Levi Strauss & Co. and some of its products. Then answer the questions.

Levi Strauss & Co.

- Can be reached by mail at P.O. Box 7215
  San Francisco, California 94120-6928.
- Was founded in 1850.
- Makes more than 5,000 different products.
- Sells its products in more than seventy countries.

Original Product: Levi 501 Jeans   Recent Product: Levi Tailored Classics

---

1. Top-selling Levi 501 jeans have remained almost exactly the same since they were created over 100 years ago. What makes these jeans so popular all over the world? Consider, for example, fabric, price, style, quality, fit, durability, and availability.

2. Look at the photo and the drawing. Do you think the man wearing Levi 501 jeans would buy Levi Tailored Classics? Why or why not?

2. Gathering Data: Using a Pie Chart

The pie chart that follows presents the results of market research conducted for Levi Strauss & Co. The company hired consultants to ask 2,000 U.S. men about their preferences in clothing. Based on their answers, the consultants concluded that every U.S. man fits into one of the five categories in the pie chart. Executives at Levi Strauss use this market research information to develop new menswear products.

A. Read the pie chart. Work in pairs. Ask and answer the questions below the chart. Then discuss your answers with the class.

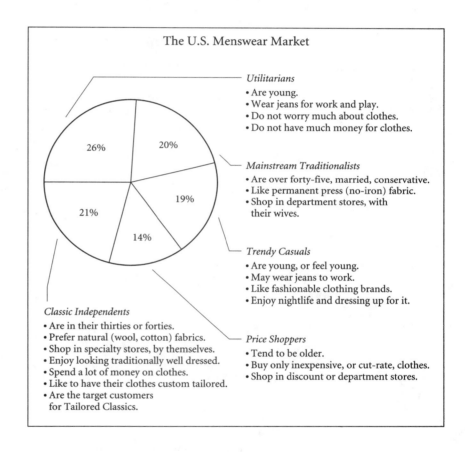

The U.S. Menswear Market

Utilitarians
• Are young.
• Wear jeans for work and play.
• Do not worry much about clothes.
• Do not have much money for clothes.

Mainstream Traditionalists
• Are over forty-five, married, conservative.
• Like permanent press (no-iron) fabric.
• Shop in department stores, with their wives.

Trendy Casuals
• Are young, or feel young.
• May wear jeans to work.
• Like fashionable clothing brands.
• Enjoy nightlife and dressing up for it.

Classic Independents
• Are in their thirties or forties.
• Prefer natural (wool, cotton) fabrics.
• Shop in specialty stores, by themselves.
• Enjoy looking traditionally well dressed.
• Spend a lot of money on clothes.
• Like to have their clothes custom tailored.
• Are the target customers for Tailored Classics.

Price Shoppers
• Tend to be older.
• Buy only inexpensive, or cut-rate, clothes.
• Shop in discount or department stores.

1. Look at the photo of the man wearing Levi 501 jeans on page 46. Which of the five categories, or segments, of the menswear market does he fit into?
2. Can the five segments in the pie chart be used to describe the menswear market in other countries? Explain.

B. Do a market survey interview of a male student. Try to determine his preferences in clothing by asking if he wears jeans and when, where he shops for clothes, how important clothes are to him, and if he shops alone or not. Then, based on his answers, decide which segment of the menswear market he fits into.

3. Gathering Data: Reading

Levi Strauss & Co. is the largest clothing manufacturer in the world. For years, the company depended on one basic product that was invented over 100 years ago: blue jeans. Now it sells over 5,000 different products, and it is always looking for new ideas.

Read these articles to gather background data on the company, including information to answer these questions:

- How did the original Mr. Levi Strauss create jeans?
- What new Levi products have succeeded or failed in recent years?
- Why does Levi Strauss & Co. continue to develop new products?

A. Scanning for Information

Work in groups of three. Look at the outline called Levi Strauss & Co. Product History on page 49. Each person should scan one of the three articles and take notes in the appropriate section of the outline. Then, share information so that everyone in your group has the same data and can fill in the Levi Strauss & Co. Product History outline completely.

1. THE CREATION OF LEVI JEANS

The life of Levi Strauss is a U.S. success story. A German who immigrated to America in 1847 at age twenty, Levi Strauss began by selling needles, thread, and buttons in New York. On the invitation of his brother-in-law, he sailed to San Francisco in 1853.

Gold had been discovered in California a few years before, and the Gold Rush had begun. The population exploded as more and more people came to try to get rich overnight. Suddenly, thousands of people started mining for gold. Strauss noticed that the miners complained that their pants were always tearing easily and that the pockets ripped apart as soon as one put a few nuggets[1] in them.

Levi Strauss saw a business opportunity. He began making pants out of some heavy brown canvas he had brought to use for tents or wagon covers. These new pants were stiff, but they sold briskly. When the original fabric was used up, Strauss sent to Europe for more. What he got was a lighter, more flexible fabric from Nîmes, France, called "serge de Nîmes." This cloth, which became known as denim, proved even more useful for pants, since it was just as strong but much more comfortable. With indigo, the pants were dyed the familiar blue color.

Miners still complained of problems with their pockets. On the advice of Nevada tailor Jacob Davis, Strauss went to a blacksmith and had the jeans pockets reinforced with metal rivets. In 1873, they patented[2] the popular innovation. The rivets, along with the patterned stitching on the hip pockets, became Levi trademarks.

Levi Strauss & Co. has continued to flourish. Since those early days, it has been a leader in the garment industry. Jeans have become desirable and even fashionable clothing for not only miners, farmers, and cowboys, but also for movie stars, executives, women, children, and teenagers from all over the world. The company is still run by descendants of Levi Strauss. Robert Haas, who heads up the Tailored Classics division, is the great-great-grandnephew of the founder. The company now markets a wide range of clothing and accessories, all under the brand name Levi's. Many new Levi products have been launched over the years. The company is still best known, however, as the maker of Levi jeans, the pants that are guaranteed to shrink[3] wrinkle, and fade[4].

1. small lumps of rock with gold
2. legally registered as company property
3. become smaller after washing
4. lose color

Levi Strauss & Co. Product History

1. The Creation of Levi Jeans

A. Levi Strauss's Early Years
  1. New York

  2. San Francisco

B. A Business Opportunity
  1. Brown canvas

  2. Blue denim

  3. Rivets

C. The Business Grows
  1. New customers

  2. New products

2. Other Levi Strauss Products

A. Flops
  1. No-iron slacks

  2. Bathing suits

  3. Sheets and towels

B. Successes
  1. Women's sportswear

  2. Growth rate

  3. Men's moderately dressy slacks and suits

C. More Product Ideas
  1. Men's dressy slacks and suits

  2. Other dressy apparel

3. Why New Products Are Needed

A. Single-Item Risk
  1. Jeans

B. Demographic Changes in U.S.
  1. Aging baby boomer generation

  2. Lower birthrate

C. Increased Competition
  1. National brands

  2. Designer brands

  3. Cut-rate brands

2. OTHER LEVI STRAUSS PRODUCTS

The original and most famous Levi Strauss product is blue jeans. Throughout its history, however, the company has researched and developed a number of other products. Some of these have succeeded beautifully, but others have flopped completely.

In 1954, flushed with the success of the cotton twill pants it had introduced a few years earlier, Levi brought out a line of permanent press (no-iron) slacks. Within six months, 5 out of every 100 pairs sold had been returned, and Levi had to admit it didn't have the right fabric for permanent press. Fifteen years later, as the company was planning its major expansion, it hit on a couple of equally dramatic flops. First was the denim bathing suit—which, when wet, weighed the wearer down to the point of imminent drowning. Next was a line of disposable (throw-away) sheets and towels. These, Levi discovered, were not high on the consumer's list of priorities. Unable to interest hotels in the product, the company was saved when the factory that made the sheets burned down. Levi absorbed the $250,000 loss.

Eventually Levi created six new divisions, ranging from jeans to accessories and including a sizable effort in women's sportswear, Levi's for Gals. The diversification[1] worked. In the mid-1970s Levi's sales hit the billion-dollar mark, having taken 125 years to reach that milestone. Four years later sales hit $2 billion. In 1979 the company ranked 167 on *Fortune*'s[2] list of the 500 largest industrial corporations, and 20 in net profits.[3] Between 1970 and 1980 Levi had grown an average of 23 percent a year. In 1979 alone it sold 143 million garments.

In menswear, though, all Levi products had been aimed at the middle of the market. The company had brought out a line of moderately dressy slacks and polyester leisure suits—the Action Slack and Action Suit—and was doing a brisk business with them. But the tempting upper end of the market remained untouched.

"If we want to grow we're probably going to have to go to upper moderate price points," one Levi official explained, "and somewhat higher taste levels for our products." In short, they needed to sell more expensive clothes—like the Tailored Classic. If Levi could sell sport coats, dress slacks, and, above all, suits, a whole new market would open up. The Tailored Classic might make money all by itself. But even more important, it would get Levi into the business of producing fancier and costlier clothing. The consumer would come to think of it as a manufacturer of dress apparel and it could spin off[4] many more such lines in the future.

1. production of very different kinds of products
2. an important U.S. business magazine
3. profits after the company pays income taxes
4. create (other related products)

3. WHY NEW PRODUCTS ARE NEEDED

Why, with such a record of success, would any company be worrying about making new products? Part of the answer, obviously, is the sheer riskiness of depending so heavily on a single item. The boom in jeans was in many ways a historical accident, and what history has given it can also take away.

Then, too, the demographics of the marketplace were already beginning to change. Jeans, to be sure, were no longer the exclusive province of youth: baby boomers[1] who had grown up on Levi's kept on wearing them into their twenties. But they would no longer be wearing them everywhere and all the time, as they did when they were teenagers. And the next generation of adolescents was not so numerous. The birthrate had peaked in 1957; by 1964, demographers agreed, the baby boom in the United States was over. The bulge in the population that the boom had created would soon be moving into a world of casual slacks, leisure suits, and coats and ties. From a marketing point of view, that's where the action would be.

Finally, the competition had been gearing up. Levi's had always shared the market with Blue Bell's Wranglers and other national brands like Lee. But now everyone seemed to be selling jeans. Back in 1970 Levi probably couldn't have forseen the popularity of "designer" jeans skimming off[2] the upper end of the market. But they could certainly anticipate cut-rate models gnawing away at the low end. To sell their wares, Levi knew, retailers would have to slash prices. The profit outlook in a saturated, competitive marketplace like this was bleak.

1. U.S. citizens born immediately after World War II (a period of high population growth)
2. taking away

B. Interpreting Information

Review the information on your Levi Strauss & Co. Product History outline. Read each statement below. Decide whether you agree or disagree. Write *agree* or *disagree* in the blank. Work in small groups. Compare your answers with those of your classmates, and explain your opinions. There is no one right answer.

1. _____ Levi Strauss & Co. should stick to manufacturing menswear products.

2. _____ Levi Strauss & Co. is known as a clothing company, so any new product should be clothing, too.

3. _____ Levi Strauss & Co. should work on varying its jeans to expand the market. For example, it should bring out a line of designer jeans with a special fit and fabric.

4. _____ The Levi company has been so successful selling jeans that it should just be content and stop trying to grow.

5. _____ In order to expand, Levi Strauss & Co. should create a new brand name. The company would manufacture the products, but they would not be called Levi's.

C. Reviewing Background Information and Vocabulary

Read the sentences and find the word or expression in the box that means the same as the italicized words. Then compare your answers with those of a classmate. If you disagree, consult another classmate, a dictionary, or your teacher.

a. greatly reduce

b. quick and active

c. very inexpensive

d. legally registered as his company's property

e. introducing

f. clothing

g. most important concerns

h. failed

i. prepared

j. recent changes of style

k. changes to fit the individual

Levi Strauss & Co. makes many products for the womenswear market.

_____ 1. When Mr. Levi Strauss first created jeans, he had no idea that he was *launching* one of the best business ideas in the history of the clothing industry.

_____ 2. The rivets on the pockets of the jeans were a special feature of the design. Mr. Strauss *patented* his invention so that it could not be copied for a number of years.

_____ 3. Levi Strauss & Co. often uses market research to guide its new product development. Independent consultants survey and interview customers to determine their buying habits and *priorities*.

_____ 4. Some new Levi Strauss products have succeeded; others have *flopped*. As the company has learned, careful market research does not guarantee success.

_____ 5. Levi Strauss & Co. was first and foremost a maker of menswear, but it has become very successful as a manufacturer of women's and children's *apparel*, too.

_____ 6. Levi Strauss & Co. expected that it would do a *brisk* business with Tailored Classics, but the new line of dressier sport coats and slacks did not sell well.

_____ 7. The designer jean market *geared up* to challenge the dominance of Levi Strauss & Co. Many companies now offer high-fashion styles that are heavily advertised.

_____ 8. According to Levi Strauss market research, customers in the Price Shopper segment of the menswear market look for *cut-rate* clothing. To these men, low price is much more important than high style.

_____ 9. Men who are in the Trendy Casual segment of the market like to follow the *trends* in fashion. They buy the latest styles and enjoy looking fashionable.

_____10. The Tailored Classics line includes ready-to-wear sport coats and slacks. The garments are designed to require no *custom tailoring*.

_____11. Tailored Classics were designed for the Classic Independent segment of the menswear market, people who do not mind spending money on clothes. When Tailored Classics did not sell well, prices were cut somewhat. Levi Strauss executives, however, did not feel they should *slash* the prices.

PART 2

MAKING DECISIONS—APPLYING MARKET RESEARCH TO NEW PRODUCT DEVELOPMENT

Introduction to the Problem. Levi Strauss & Co. has always tried to expand by developing new products and new markets. As the population of those who wear jeans grows older, the company has tried to make dressier, costlier clothing like Tailored Classics to sell to these customers. The problem is that, so far, Classic Independents, those who enjoy spending money on nice clothes, have not been interested in Tailored Classics.

Keep the problem in mind as you do the following exercises.

4. Exploring Business Culture: New Product Development

Read each statement about a business practice related to new product development at Levi Strauss & Co. Then, check [✔] whether you consider them usual or unusual business practices. In small groups, compare your answers and discuss the ones you have checkmarked as unusual.

Aspects of a New Product Development at Levi Strauss

	Usual	Unusual
1. There is a continual search year after year for new product ideas.		
2. Extensive and costly market research precedes new product development.		
3. Market research is often carried out by independent consultants who are hired by the company.		
4. New products share the same brand name as older ones, though their markets may be very different.		
5. If a new product does not succeed in the first selling season, it is abandoned.		

5. Strategies for Negotiation: Expressing Disagreement and Doubt

As a participant in business meetings, you need to be able to express your disagreement or doubt clearly. One way to disagree politely, but clearly, is to make statements about your feelings with *I* or *we*. This strategy is good because it makes people less defensive. They do not perceive your comment as a personal attack.

Here are some expressions you can use to express disagreement or doubt:

> *I'm concerned that...*
>
> *Maybe we need to look at...*
>
> *I'm not completely convinced...*

1. **Prepare to use the negotiating strategy. Write the expressions in the box on cards or strips of paper. Use the expressions in the exercise below.**

2. **Work in small groups. Discuss one or more of these situations. When you want to express disagreement or doubt, use an expression from your cards.**

   a. Some Levi Strauss executives want to work with a major European clothing designer to create an elegant new line of designer Levi jeans. The new line would have a double name: (Designer's Name) Levi's. Is this a good idea?

   b. Imagine that you all work for the same company. An important business associate is coming to visit the city where you work. The person will be in town for twenty-four hours. What should you do?

   - One of you would like to demonstrate your ability to control costs by choosing a modest hotel and inviting the guest to dinner at your home.

   - Another would like to impress the person with the best hotel, restaurant, and entertainment your city can offer.

   - Still another thinks it best to ask the guest for his or her preferences.

6. Conducting a Business Meeting: A Division Meeting

A. Preparing for the Meeting

1. **Read about the business problem.**

   Robert Haas, director of the Tailored Classics division, is anxiously seeking ways to improve Tailored Classics sales, which are terrible in this first selling season. If this new product line flops, people in the division may lose salary increases or even their jobs.

   - Why are Tailored Classics selling so poorly?

   - What changes can we make to increase sales?

2. Notice the format of the meeting.

Introduction

- Robert Haas, director of the Tailored Classics division and great-great-grandnephew of Levi Strauss, opens the meeting by welcoming and introducing everyone.
- Mr. Haas states the purpose of the meeting: to analyze problems with the troubled Tailored Classics line and identify changes to increase sales.

Agenda

- Each group meets to discuss the problem from its point of view. Haas moves around the room and listens in on the groups.
- Haas invites all participants to analyze the Tailored Classics problem and offer suggestions for solving it. When appropriate, participants express disagreement and doubt.

Closing

- Haas summarizes the main recommendations made during the meeting.
- He closes the meeting by thanking everyone, and says that he will decide what steps to take by close of business tomorrow.

3. Review your notes on the Levi Strauss & Co. Product History outline, the vocabulary, the information on business culture, and the negotiating strategy in the unit. Prepare to use this information in the meeting.

B. Conducting the Meeting

Role play the division meeting.

- Select one person to run the meeting as Robert Haas. Mr. Haas will begin the meeting and follow the format described.
- Form two groups of Levi Strauss executives and one group of consultants. Read the role summaries on pages 56 and 57. Follow the meeting format described.

The Roles

Top Managers for the Tailored Classics Division

You believe you have a great product that was developed with careful market research. Everyone in the division simply has to work harder to sell the line. You want to emphasize that:

- Sales people must be more aggressive. They have to get department store managers to make special displays and talk about the line to customers.

- Advertising has to be more creative. It must show the Classic Independents that Levi Strauss & Co. can make stylish sport coats and slacks.

- Prices may have to be cut further, at least for this selling season.

- *(Add your own.)*

Line Managers for the Tailored Classics Division

Each of you has worked hard for the new product, but you disagree with or have serious doubts about some of the business decisions that have been made by the top managers. You want to express the following concerns:

- Advertising concerns: You have tried to create an elegant image for Levi Tailored Classics, but you are convinced that this image does not fit the Levi Strauss brand name.

- Sales concerns: You have sent your sales representatives to the department stores that always sell Levi's, but you know that Classic Independents do not usually shop there.

- Design and Production concern: You were told to design Tailored Classics to require no custom tailoring, but Classic Independents like to have their clothing tailored.

- *(Add your own.)*

> **Market Research Consultants**
>
> You were hired by Levi Strauss executives to do the market research on which the product is based. You believe that the Levi Strauss executives have targeted the right market, Classic Independents, but have designed the wrong product for these customers. You want to point out that:
>
> - Classic Independents enjoy shopping in specialty stores that sell expensive and distinctive clothing, and they do not mind paying for it.
> - They prefer natural fabrics to polyester and wool blends.
> - These men want custom-tailored clothes not ready-to-wear apparel like Tailored Classics.
> - They do not think that the company can make dressy apparel. To them, Levi Strauss & Co. means sportswear.
> - *(Add your own.)*

7. Follow-Up Activities

A. Business Writing

Write an interoffice letter to Robert Haas, director of the Tailored Classics division. State the main reasons for low sales of Tailored Classics and what steps the division should take to solve the problem.

For a model of an interoffice letter, see page 42.

B. Putting the Problem in Perspective: Applying Business Concepts

1. **Read the summary below. Comment on the quality of Levi Strauss's business decisions.**

Levi Strauss's Continuing Search for New Products

Levi Strauss & Co. remains a leader in the garment industry because the company continues to launch new products that create trends and adapt to the market.

Some years ago, Levi Strauss & Co., makers of the famous pants that are guaranteed to shrink, wrinkle, and fade, was not earning the kind of profits it expected in the U.S. market. The jeans market was *saturated* with competing brands at all price levels, and these competitors were skimming off profits. Moreover, the *demographics* of the jeans market were changing dramatically: The children of the 1950s—baby boomers—were growing older, putting on weight, and buying more office clothing than jeans. The Levi Strauss company needed to find products to appeal to different kinds of customers.

Over the years, one of the company's priorities had been to *diversify* by producing products very different from jeans. Its *diversification* efforts in women's sportswear had been successful. The Levi's for Gals division, for example, had consistently high sales. The company had also been able to *spin off* many other products for these women customers, ranging from accessories to jackets. After extensive market research on the buying habits of U.S. men, Levi Strauss & Co. identified a new, clothes-conscious segment of the market, which it named Classic Independents. To appeal to these men, the company developed

Tailored Classics. However, this new line failed to attract the better-dressed menswear customers that Levi Strauss had *targeted*. Tailored Classics ran into problems of fabric, price, image, and distribution.

Later the company tried again to enter the upper end of the men's apparel market with a line created in cooperation with Perry Ellis, a major American designer. This idea also flopped. It was not until recently that Levi Strauss & Co. brought out a successful new menswear line, Dockers. Instead of designing for the Classic Independents, the company *targeted* other segments of the market with medium-priced clothing that is only slightly dressier than jeans. The look is casual, the fit is relaxed, and sales are brisk.

2. Answer the questions based on what you have learned. Use the italicized expressions in your answers.

a. A *saturated* market is one that has enough products at a certain price and quality level so that it is not profitable to introduce similar products. Is the jeans market *saturated* in your area? Could Levi Strauss & Co. expand there?

b. The characteristics of a particular group of people are called its *demographics*. Describe the *demographics* of the jeans market in your area. Consider age, gender, size of the population, and economic status. Are the *demographics* of this market changing?

c. *Diversification* is the production of different kinds of products (and/or the acquisition of other companies that produce such products) as a strategy to reduce risk and gain markets. Why is *diversification* necessary for Levi Strauss & Co.? Do all companies need to *diversify* in order to stay profitable?

d. *Spin offs* are related products created to build on the success of an earlier product. What *spin offs* of Levi's jeans are you familiar with? Have you bought any of these products?

e. When a company identifies a market and tries to sell especially to it, this is called *targeting* a market. Why did the Levi Strauss & Co. plan to *target* the Classic Independents market with Tailored Classics fail? Which segments of the menswear market has the company *targeted* with Dockers?

C. Fieldwork

Report to the class on Levi Strauss products in your area.

- Go to several medium-priced clothing stores nearby.
- Ask if any Levi Strauss products are available for men and/or women.
- Find out what similar products made by other manufacturers are sold in the stores.

STEW LEONARD'S DAIRY STORE

Satisfying the Supermarket Customer

U n i t 5

Author's Note   *Stew Leonard pleaded guilty to what the* New York Times *called "the largest computer-driven tax-evasion case in the nation" shortly after this unit was written. He was sentenced to more than four years in federal prison, and he agreed to pay the government $15 million in back taxes, penalties, and interest. This does not diminish Stew Leonard's genius for customer service and retail sales, but it may illustrate the perils of success.*

PART 1

BACKGROUND

1. Examining the Products

Read the information and look at the photographs in order to become familiar with Stew Leonard's Dairy Store and its products. Then answer the questions.

Stew Leonard's Dairy Store
- Is located at 100 Westport Avenue
  Norwalk, Connecticut 06851.
- Was established in 1969.
- Has 650 employees.
- Has annual sales of $100 million.

Stew Leonard stands outside his 115,000-square-foot dairy store (32,323 square meters) with two employees dressed in animal costumes to entertain customers. The fruit and vegetable department as well as the complete in-store bakery are pictured here. The store also has large dairy and fish departments. Stew Leonard's Dairy Store is open from 7 A.M. to 11 P.M. every day except December 25, Christmas.

1. Stew Leonard and his family own and operate a very large and profitable supermarket. Compare Stew Leonard's Dairy Store to supermarkets you are familiar with. Consider, for example, entertainment, food departments, store size, and hours of business.
2. Would you like to buy your groceries here? Why, or why not?

2. Gathering Data: Listening

You will hear Stew Leonard and one of his associates describe the Stew Leonard approach to supermarket sales. This unusual approach combines efficiency, customer service, and fun. The approach works: An average of 100,000 shoppers buy $2 million worth of groceries at the store each week.

A.   Read the questions. Then listen to the tape and write your answers. Compare your responses with those of a classmate. If you disagree, listen again.

1. According to Stew Leonard, what is the relationship between the quantity (volume of sales), quality, and price of food he sells in the store?

_____

_____

2. One of Stew Leonard's principles is efficiency. In what ways is the store efficient?

_____

_____

3. Another business principle is to limit the number of items sold in the store. Stew Leonard says that 20 percent of the items in a supermarket bring 80 percent of the sales. How has he used this information to design his business?

_____

_____

4. How many items does Stew Leonard stock? What are the advantages and disadvantages of selling fewer items?

_____

_____

B.   Discuss your reactions to the tape about Stew Leonard. Did anything surprise or interest you particularly? What do you think of his approach to doing business?

3. Gathering Data: Reading

Stew Leonard has been very successful in the competitive U.S. supermarket business. In addition to high profits, he has won high praise, including the Presidential Award for Entrepreneurial Achievement and an Honorary Doctorate of Business from the University of Bridgeport (Connecticut). He approaches the often dull but necessary business of buying and selling groceries with creativity and fun.

Read these articles to gather background data on the company, including information to answer these questions:

* How did Stew Leonard get started in the grocery business?
* What are the secrets of his success in this business?

Work in groups of three. Look at the Stew Leonard's Fact Sheet on page 64. Each person should scan one of the three articles and take notes in the appropriate section of the outline. Then, share the information so that everyone in your group has the same data and can fill in the Stew Leonard's Fact Sheet completely.

1. BEGINNING THE BUSINESS

In Connecticut, a northeastern state near New York, Stew Leonard's father was the owner of a small dairy. He used to take Stew along when he delivered milk to families in the morning. From childhood, Stew Leonard remembers wanting to be somebody, wanting to be noticed and appreciated. Perhaps it had something to do with being the sixth out of seven children. After studying dairy manufacturing at the University of Connecticut, Stew Leonard assumed he would go into a partnership with his father. But his father died suddenly, and Stew found himself taking over the family business with his brother.

Fifteen years later, unexpected circumstances caused another change: The state put a highway right through the land where the dairy was located. Stew surveyed customers to see what they wanted, and he visited other small dairies to find out how they were doing. The farmer who was bottling and selling his milk on the premises,[1] rather than selling it to a middleman[2] was doing well, while many of the old-fashioned dairies were going under. Stew Leonard decided to redesign his dairy business to suit the changing times and his personality.

More than door-to-door service, Stew Leonard found out that customers wanted good milk prices. So, he ended deliveries and instead created a factory-outlet[3] dairy store. He bought raw milk from farmers in huge quantities, processed it in a glass-enclosed plant in the middle of the store and sold it in standard half-gallon (1.8 liter) cartons with his name and a picture of a cow on them. His slogan was, "You'd have to own a cow to get fresher milk."

As the business grew, he created more and more of a Disneyland Dairy Store where customers might come and bring their children to be entertained. As Leonard remarks, "Where children go, their mothers will follow." Not long after, he began adding to his original list of eight products and enlarging the building until it became, as proclaimed on the building, "the world's largest dairy store."

1. in the building
2. a distributor who handles goods between the producer and the consumer
3. discount store selling large quantities of products

2. BUSINESS PRINCIPLE: SUPERMARKET SHOPPING SHOULD BE FUN

To Stew Leonard, the distinction between a supermarket and an amusement park is slight, and not necessarily useful.

"Everyone feels supermarket shopping is drudgery,[1]" Mr. Leonard said in an interview in his office overlooking the selling floor. "I try to make it fun."

Mr. Leonard clearly has the most fun greeting customers, and most are delighted to see him. As he made his way through the produce[2] section during the interview, Dr. Shelley Dreisman of Westport, Connecticut, happily shook his hand, but her daughter, Emily, age six, shyly turned away. "She only wants to shake hands with the cow," Dr. Dreisman explained.

That cow, it turns out, is often Mr. Leonard, too. When the burdens of running a $100 million business seem too great, he puts on a cow suit he keeps in his office closet and goes out and hugs customers. . . .

Outside the store, in the parking lot, there is a petting zoo, a collection of live barnyard animals including geese, calves, baby goats, and sheep.

Even the petting zoo serves several purposes. Mr. Leonard talks of it as an afterthought. When he sought to buy the property twenty years ago, the elderly woman who owned it insisted on keeping her farm animals on it.

Now, farmers lend him baby animals, which he periodically exchanges for younger models. The farmers like the arrangement, he said, because the animals come back well fed. Mr. Leonard pays for part of their diet, but the animals also get food from shoppers, who buy it in the store.

1. unpleasant work
2. fruits and vegetables

Stew Leonard's Fact Sheet

1. Beginning the Business

A. The Leonard Family Dairy
   1. Stew's father

   2. Stew's childhood and youth

B. Changing Times
   1. New roads

   2. New kinds of dairies

C. Designing the Dairy Store
   1. Factory-outlet store

   2. Disneyland store

2. Business Principle: Supermarket Shopping Should Be Fun

A. Stew Leonard's Role
   1. Greeting customers

   2. Entertaining customers

B. The Petting Zoo
   1. History

   2. Business purposes

3. Business Principle: Listen to the Customer

A. Ways of Eliciting Suggestions

B. The Strawberry Suggestion
   1. A change in packaging

   2. Advantages and disadvantages

   3. Effect on sales

C. The Turkey Suggestions
   1. A change in packaging; effect on sales

   2. A further change in packaging; effect on sales

3. BUSINESS PRINCIPLE: LISTEN TO THE CUSTOMER

Stew Leonard elicits opinions from his supermarket customers through monthly customer interviews, called focus groups, and a suggestion box. Every day over 100 suggestions are received, typed up, and distributed to the appropriate departments. He tries out many of these suggestions, even if they seem unlikely.

According to Mr. Leonard, two recent successes came from customer ideas put into the suggestion box.

One was to sell strawberries loose, like tomatoes, in the big flat trays from the farm, not in plastic one-pint (0.551 liter) baskets.

The produce manager said that if the strawberries were set out loose, people would eat them and the leftovers would never sell. He turned out to be right, but customers who can choose strawberries individually will drop them into plastic bags without watching the total, Mr. Leonard discovered, and some will buy twelve dollars worth. Sales tripled.

Then there were the turkey dinners. Mr. Leonard was selling them with vegetable and stuffing,[1] fresh but refrigerated, at $5.95 each, and roasting just three turkeys a day in the store's kitchens to keep up with demand. A customer suggested selling them at the hot-food bar,[2] a growing part of the business; so he did, and demand jumped to twenty-one turkeys a day.

But some customers said they did not like paying $2.99 a pound

Stew Leonard's rock of commitment states the store's policy of satisfying the customer. All customers walk by this rock as they enter the store. Why is the policy written in stone?

for the gravy mixed in, or that the gravy had too many calories. Others said there was not enough gravy. So he started putting the gravy on the side,[3] and demand rose to more than fifty turkeys a day.

1. filling made of bread and spices
2. area inside the store where hot food is sold
3. in a separate container

B. Interpreting Information

Review the information on your Stew Leonard's Fact Sheet. Read each statement below. Decide whether you agree or disagree with it. Write *agree* or *disagree* in the blank. Work in small groups. Compare your answers with those of your classmates, and explain your opinions. There is no one right answer.

_____ 1. Stew Leonard learned the dairy business from his father.

_____ 2. Too much entertainment in a supermarket could decrease sales.

_____ 3. Stew Leonard's shoppers probably include more families than single or elderly people.

_____ 4. Price is more important than entertainment in attracting shoppers that will consistently return to a supermarket.

_____ 5. Employees at Stew Leonard's probably work harder than those at other large supermarkets.

_____ 6. When sales are slow, Stew Leonard's is less likely to pay attention to customer suggestions.

C. Reviewing Background Information and Vocabulary

Read the sentences and find the word or expression in the box that means the same as the italicized words. Then compare your answers with those of a classmate. If you disagree, consult another classmate, a dictionary, or your teacher.

a. rise

b. brought into the store and immediately sold

c. supposing

d. unpleasant work

e. be respected by others

f. in the building

g. to individual houses

h. regularly offers for sale

i. a later and less important idea

j. going bankrupt

_____ 1. When Stew Leonard was a child, he had a strong desire to *be somebody*. He wanted to do important work in the community.

_____ 2. Stew Leonard's father owned a dairy and had a milk route. He delivered bottles of milk *door-to-door*.

_____ 3. As a young man growing up, Stew admired his father. Stew studied dairy manufacturing, *assuming* that he would go into the family business with his father.

_____ 4. When the state built a highway through his property, Stew looked around at other small dairies in the area. He noticed that many of them were *going under*, so he decided to make some changes.

_____ 5. Stew decided to build a dairy that could become a tourist attraction. He would bottle milk, sell it and entertain people right *on the premises*.

_____ 6. Little by little, the dairy store grew into a supermarket with entertainment. Stew Leonard wanted customers and their children to think of grocery shopping as fun, not *drudgery*.

_____ 7. He planned many of the entertaining features of the store, but the petting zoo came as *an afterthought*. It is now one of the most popular attractions for children.

_____ 8. Stew Leonard's store *stocks* only about 700 items, while the typical U.S. grocery store may have 15,000. The idea is to sell a lot of each item. This keeps the prices down and builds customer loyalty.

_____ 9. To keep prices low and quality high, Stew buys truckloads of produce directly from farmers. These items are *turned over* quickly.

_____10. Customers urged him to let them choose their own strawberries, instead of buying them in prepacked baskets. This change caused sales to *jump* dramatically.

PART 2

MAKING DECISIONS—SATISFYING THE SUPERMARKET CUSTOMER

Introduction to the Problem. Stew Leonard has created an exceptionally profitable supermarket by generating high-volume sales of quality food at good prices. His success is also built on a policy of satisfying the customer, which creates a high degree of customer loyalty. But some customers are clearly not happy. Is it possible to satisfy all of them?

Keep the question in mind as you do the exercises.

4. Exploring Business Culture: Supermarket Sales

Read each group of statements about a business practice related to the supermarket business. Decide whether you consider the idea usual or unusual. Write *usual* or *unusual* in the blank. In small groups, compare your answers and discuss the ones labeled *unusual*.

Stew Leonard's Approach to Supermarket Sales

Dealing with Customers
— 1. "Our mission is to create happy customers."
— 2. "The customer who complains is our friend."
— 3. "It's five times harder to find a new customer than it is to keep an old one."

Marketing the Product
— 4. "Lower the price and sell the best. Word of mouth (personal recommendations) will do the rest."
— 5. "Pile it (the product) high and watch them buy."
— 6. "If you wouldn't take it home to your mother, don't put it out for our customers."

Stew Leonard

Managing Employees
— 7. "Hire people more for their attitudes than for their skills or intelligence."
— 8. "Management by appreciation: appreciate your customers, employees, and suppliers."

5. Strategies for Negotiation: Building on Someone Else's Idea

As a business manager, you need to be able to listen to and work with other people's ideas. One person's thought might inspire other thoughts. Systematic development of ideas can encourage teamwork. It can also be an important strategy in negotiations and meetings of all kinds.

Here are some expressions you can use to build on someone else's idea:

> *And, to add to your idea...*
>
> *And, what if...*
>
> *Yes, and...*

1. Prepare to use the negotiating strategy. Write the expressions in the box on cards or strips of paper. Use these phrases in the exercise below.

2. **Work in small groups. Discuss one or more of these situations. Give your own ideas and opinions. When you want to build on someone else's idea, use an expression from your cards.**

a. An employee from the Fish Department is offering samples of smoked salmon, an expensive new item, to customers in the store. Instead of taking one sample, a customer from a nearby factory comes in and stops to eat lunch on the samples. What should the employee do?

b. There is a profit problem in the Ice Cream Shop at Stew Leonard's store. Some supervisors suspect that employees working there are giving out free ice cream cones to their friends. What should the supervisors do?

6. Conducting a Business Meeting: A Customer Focus Group

A. Preparing for the Meeting

1. **Read about the business problem.**

Stew Leonard's Dairy Store owes a great deal of its success to customers' suggestions. The idea that "the customer is always right" is an essential business policy, yet it does cause problems for store executives. Today Stew Leonard is conducting one of his monthly focus group meetings with customers and managers to determine what they do not like. He and his managers have to find ways of answering some difficult suggestions from loyal customers.

2. **Notice the format of the meeting.**

Introduction
- To open the meeting, Stew Leonard, president, welcomes and introduces everyone.
- He states the purpose of the meeting: to listen to customers' suggestions and work together to find appropriate responses.

Agenda
- Each of the three groups meets separately to review its role. Stew Leonard moves around the room and listens in on the groups.
- Mr. Leonard then begins the focus group. He asks each customer, "What don't you like about the store?" He invites all the managers to respond to the suggestions. Whenever possible, participants build on each other's ideas to come up with responses.

Closing

- To close the meeting, Stew Leonard summarizes what action the store will take regarding each suggestion.

- He thanks the customers for participating, offers each one a twenty-dollar store certificate and mentions that each suggestion will receive a written reply.

3. Review your notes on Stew Leonard's Fact Sheet, the vocabulary, the information on business culture, and the negotiating strategy of the unit. Prepare to use this information in the meeting.

B. Conducting the Meeting

Role play the focus group.

- Select one person to run the focus group as Stew Leonard, president. He will begin the meeting and follow the format described above.

- Form three groups, top managers, department managers, and loyal customers. Read the role summaries here and on pages 70 and 71. Follow the meeting format described.

The Roles

Top Managers at Stew Leonard's Dairy Store

You believe that your business depends on satisfying as many customers as possible.

- Your competition is ninety-three other food stores within a ten-mile circle around the store.

- You have about 100,000 customers per week parking their 50,000 automobiles in your parking lot.

- You know, as Stew Leonard says, "It's five times harder to find a new customer than it is to keep an old one."

Department Managers at Stew Leonard's Dairy Store

You are all very proud of the quantity and quality of items you sell. You believe in satisfying the customer, but you also have some limitations. Use the information below to help you respond to customer suggestions.

Bakery Department

- Is located at the store entrance to greet customers with a pleasant aroma.
- Sells 10,000 loaves of bread and 75,000 croissants every week, more than any in-store bakery.
- Must sell 2,000 of any item weekly to guarantee freshness.

Dairy Department

- Bottles milk on the premises in a glass-enclosed milk-processing plant.
- Packages by machine 9,000 standard half-gallons of milk per hour (1/2 gallon = 1.9 liter).
- Sells weekly 96,000 half-gallons of milk and 4.8 tons of butter (1 ton = .9 metric ton).

Fish Department

- Packages fish on the premises, and fills some individual orders.
- Brings fresh fish from New York and Boston fish markets daily.
- Sells weekly 3,000 pounds of fillet of sole and 6,000 pounds of shrimp (1 lb. = .45 kilo).

Produce Department

- Creates huge, attractive displays of fresh fruit and vegetables in the store.
- Brings truckloads of fresh produce directly from California and local farmers.
- Sells weekly such quantities as 150,000 ears of corn and 36,000 pounds of bananas.

> **Loyal Customers of Stew Leonard's Dairy Store**
>
> Each of you has a suggestion for the store managers. Choose one complaint from the list below. Discuss possible actions you want Stew Leonard's store to take.
>
> Suggestion 1: "The fish bothers me. You say it's fresh, but you sell it in plastic supermarket packages. It doesn't look fresh."
>
> Suggestion 2: "My four kids and I used to enjoy your cranberry nut muffins, but now you've stopped making them. Why discontinue a good product?"
>
> Suggestion 3: "The strawberries trucked in from California just don't have any taste. They look good, but I'm always disappointed."
>
> Suggestion 4: "I live in the senior citizen housing next door and like to shop here. Your milk is very good, but I need smaller cartons. Half-gallons are too big for me."
>
> Suggestion 5: "I like the store a lot, but it's an hour's drive for my family. Why not build more stores, including one closer to New York City?"
>
> Suggestion 6: "I've been a customer for fifteen years. Last month my car was dented by a shopping cart in your overcrowded parking lot. I think you should pay the $2,000 repair bill."

7. Follow-Up Activities

A. Business Writing

Choose one of the following topics.

1. Write a letter to one of Stew Leonard's loyal customers from Exercise 6. Explain what action will be taken as a result of his or her suggestion. If no action will be taken, explain why. For a model of a business letter, see page 28.

2. Write a suggestion to Stew Leonard. Mention an item or service that is lacking in the store and give reasons why the store should provide it. Request a response to your suggestion.

This is a suggestion box form with Stew Leonard's photo on it.

B. Putting the Problem in Perspective and Applying Business Concepts

1. Read the summary below. Comment on the quality of Stew Leonard's business decisions.

Satisfying the Supermarket Customer

Stew Leonard has managed to make extraordinary profits in the highly competitive U.S. supermarket industry by redesigning the business in significant ways. Executives of the company summarize their approach to business in the name of its founder: *S-T-E-W*. *S* stands for Satisfy the Customer, *T* for Teamwork, *E* for Excellence and Quality, and *W* for Wow!

S is for Satisfy the Customer. Stew Leonard's approach to *customer service* is distinctive. One customer, after complaining that the steak was tough, was given not only a new steak but a bouquet of roses. As the rock of commitment at the store entrance says, "The customer is always right."

T is for teamwork. The first team is the family. The Leonard family has over twenty of its members working for the company, and over half of the employees have a relative working for the company. Teamwork goes beyond family, though, to become a way of working with the customer and with other employees. In fact, nobody talks about "employees" at Stew Leonard's; everyone is a "team member."

E is for Excellence and Quality. Instead of the typical 12,000-item supermarket, Stew Leonard's Dairy Store *inventory* includes only about 700 top-selling items. With a state-of-the-art computer system, executives can track individual items and then make adjustments in order to increase sales. Besides reducing the number of products he sells, Stew Leonard has brought a *factory-outlet* model to the supermarket. *Produce* is purchased directly from the growers. Such items as milk and bread are produced and packaged right on the premises. Both of these practices eliminate costly *handling* by *middlemen* and *distributors.* The store makes money because it sells a high *volume* of each high-quality product at a competitive price.

W is for Wow! Stew Leonard is the first to tell you that he has learned a lot about business from Disneyland. The founder of this store is a showman at heart whose motto is "Show and Sell." From the beginning, he wanted to blend entertainment with shopping and eliminate the drudgery. There is Wow! in the huge displays, the entertainment, and in the crowds of happy customers.

Despite its success, few supermarkets have imitated the *S-T-E-W* model so far. The factory-outlet specializing in one type of merchandise is transforming other industries, however. Toys "R" Us, for example, has overtaken a big share of the toy market with this approach. If you ask Stew Leonard why so few supermarkets imitate his, he will say that running this kind of business takes a lot of hard work.

2. Answer the questions based on what you have learned. Use the italicized expressions in your answers.

a. How important is *customer service* in the supermarket industry in your country? Is entertainment part of that service? Would people enjoy being entertained at the supermarket?

b. Is the *factory-outlet* model used by any industries in your country? Would people like to buy their groceries in one store that carries bread, fish, meat and produce piled up in huge displays?

c. Think about the *produce* you eat. Where does it come from? How much *handling* by how many *middlemen* does it receive? Does your market buy it from farmers or from a *distributor*?

d. Stew Leonard's dairy store's *inventory* includes few items but large quantities of each item. How do most supermarkets in your country manage their *inventory*? Is *volume* of sales or product quality more important?

C. Fieldwork

Report to your class on a large supermarket nearby.

- Visit the store to observe how it is arranged and operated.

- Interview the store manager or a department manager. Ask about store policies on dealing with customers, marketing the products, and managing employees. Ask the managers whether they agree with Stew Leonard's approach. Use Exercise 4 as a guide.

- Compare the data you collect with what you know about Stew Leonard's Dairy Store.

AIRBUS INDUSTRIE AND THE BOEING COMPANY

Negotiating International Trade Agreements

Unit **6**

BACKGROUND

1. Examining the Products

Read the information and look at the photographs to become familiar with Airbus and Boeing and some of their products. Then answer the questions.

Airbus Industrie

- Is located at 1 Rond-Point Maurice Bellonte
  31707 Blagnac Cedex
  France.
- Produces aircraft for civil purposes.
- Is a consortium of airframe manufacturers from France, Germany, Great Britain, and Spain.

Airbus *A340*

The Boeing Company

- Is located at 7755 East Marginal Way South
  Seattle, Washington 98108
  USA.
- Produces aircraft for civil and military purposes.
- Is a privately owned company.

Boeing *747*

1. Commercial airlines are the customers for these planes. The Boeing and Airbus companies have many similar products. If you were president of a commercial carrier, how would you choose which planes to order?

2. U.S. airlines purchase almost half of all of the aircraft sold worldwide. Most of the customers buy from Boeing. If you were an Airbus official, how would you get U.S. carriers to buy your European-made planes?

3. What do you know about the competition between Airbus and Boeing?

4. When you fly, are you aware of which company made the aircraft? Should you be aware?

2. Gathering Data: Using a Graph

This graph will help you understand the intense international competition between Airbus, the European consortium, and Boeing, the private U.S. company. It also shows the limited competition offered by three other airframe manufacturers. All these companies want to sell their planes to the world's airlines.

A.   Study the graph below. Working in pairs, answer the questions below the chart.

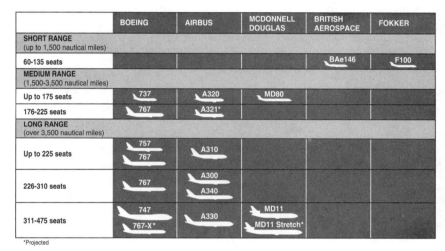

	BOEING	AIRBUS	MCDONNELL DOUGLAS	BRITISH AEROSPACE	FOKKER
SHORT RANGE (up to 1,500 nautical miles)					
60-135 seats				BAe146	F100
MEDIUM RANGE (1,500-3,500 nautical miles)					
Up to 175 seats	737	A320	MD80		
176-225 seats	767	A321*			
LONG RANGE (over 3,500 nautical miles)					
Up to 225 seats	757 / 767	A310			
226-310 seats	767	A300 / A340			
311-475 seats	747 / 767-X*	A330	MD11 / MD11 Stretch*		

*Projected

An increasingly <u>scrappy</u>[1] Airbus prepares to <u>go nose to nose</u>[2] with Boeing.

1. Notice that the graph compares airplanes in three range categories: short, medium, and long range. Describe the competition between Boeing and Airbus aircraft in each of the three ranges.

2. How will the *A321*, a medium-range airplane, help Airbus?

3. How will the *767-X*, a long-range airplane, help Boeing?

4. Look at the data on the graph about three other airframe companies: McDonnell Douglas, British Aerospace, and Fokker, which is an associate of Airbus Industrie. Their products compete only in certain categories, or market niches. In which market niches do their planes compete with Boeing and Airbus planes?

5. The most intense competition occurs in the long-range plane category. Why are the 311- to 475-seat long-range passenger planes so popular?

B.   Discuss your reaction to the chart. Does anything surprise or interest you in particular? In which market niches do you predict the most heated competition over the next ten to fifteen years?

[1] aggressive
[2] compete in each product category

3. Gathering Data: Reading

The airframe industry is one of the controversial trade issues between the European Community (EC) and the United States. There have been many rounds of trade talks.

Read these articles to gather background data for the latest round of negotiations, including information to answer these questions:

- What is the history of Airbus Industrie and the Boeing Company?
- What is the nature of the competition between the two companies?
- How does the United States differ from the European Community on the issue of government involvement in the aircraft industry?

A. Scanning for Information

Work in pairs. Look at the outline called Airbus and Boeing: A Brief Comparison on p. 80. Each person should scan one of the articles and take notes in the appropriate section of the outline. Then, share information so that you and your partner have the same data and can fill in the Airbus and Boeing outline completely.

1. AIRBUS INDUSTRIE

In 1970, four European nations created Airbus Industrie to offset[1] a decline in the airframe industry and challenge U.S. dominance in the global commercial aircraft market. Airbus is a four-country international consortium: Deutsche Airbus of Germany, with 37.9 percent ownership, makes the fuselage;[2] British Aerospace of Great Britain, with 20 percent, makes the wings; Construcciones Aeronáuticas (CASA) of Spain, with 4.2 percent, makes the tail; and Aerospatiale of France, with 37.9 percent, assembles the planes in a gigantic facility at Toulouse-Blagnac international airport. In this unusual business structure, the four partners are both owners and suppliers, the common language of business is English, and all sales are transacted in U.S. dollars.

In the early years, Airbus Industrie was clearly the underdog, lagging far behind the U.S. companies of Boeing and McDonnell Douglas, which had dominated the industry for years. Since the consortium had no track record on safety or maintenance, airlines were reluctant to purchase the new aircraft. Through favorable pricing, generous maintenance contracts, and other competitive offers, the company was able to attract a number of carriers, including some in the United States. As a result, in less than twenty years, Airbus was able to produce a full family of airplanes and, with over 100 customers, it moved into the number two spot in the global aircraft industry.

Airbus succeeds because civil aircraft manufacturers from four nations pool their financial and technological resources in a true multinational partnership. It also succeeds because officials in these countries believe that European industry must be supported and protected by a strong industrial policy. For Airbus Industrie, the largest single industrial undertaking in the EC, support takes the form of an estimated $26 billion in subsidies.[3] As a result of this financial backing, Airbus has been able to recover from 70 to 100 percent of its product development costs, which are enormous in the industry. It can easily take four to six years, for example, for a plane to move from the design stage to actual production. During this time, the project yields no profits. Government subsidies also compensate for losses from discount pricing, a strategy Airbus officials felt was necessary in order to gain a foothold[4] in the all-important U.S. market for aircraft.

Airbus officials defend subsidies as a way to help level the playing field.[5] They are quick to point out that Boeing and McDonnell Douglas receive millions of dollars in contracts to build military aircraft and spacecraft for the U.S. government, which is clearly a form of subsidy. It is hypocritical, say Airbus executives, to argue that the market is or can be completely free from government intervention.

Airbus officials point out that the consortium is a source of pride for the European Community, a model of international cooperation that can inspire future economic development in the area. Moreover, high quality Airbus products provide a viable alternative to U.S. airframes, assuring customers all over the world of the benefits of industrial competition.

With 30 percent of the global airframe market already, Airbus officials are gunning for at least 40 percent over the next several years. Predictions of increasing worldwide air traffic are fueling Airbus's growth. The consortium is already anticipating the need for airplanes that are quieter, more fuel efficient, and more comfortable for air travelers on long trips. According to company literature, "Airbus Industrie looks forward to lasting financial success well into the twenty-first century."

1. stop
2. main body of an aircraft
3. government funds
4. begin to compete
5. let competitors compete on a fair and equal basis

Airbus and Boeing: A Brief Comparison

1. Airbus Industrie

A. Company History

   1. Goals

   2. Four-nation consortium

B. Competitive Record

   1. The early phase

   2. The next phase

C. Airbus and the Four Governments

   1. Amount of subsidies to Airbus

   2. Reasons for subsidies

D. Predictions for the Future

2. The Boeing Company

A. Company History

   1. Bill Boeing

   2. Product lines

B. Competitive Record

   1. Traditional dominance

   2. New competition

C. Boeing and the U.S. Government

   1. Traditional free-market advocates

   2. New industrial policy advocates

D. Predictions for the Future

2. THE BOEING COMPANY

The Boeing Company was founded by Bill Boeing, a wealthy lumberman from Washington State, on the West Coast of the U.S. The first plane was used to take him on fishing trips to remote areas of Canada. In 1916, he set up an airplane factory in Seattle, Washington, a city which now depends on the aircraft industry. Fascinated with the technology of flying, Bill Boeing when he founded the company promised "to let no new improvement in flying and flying equipment pass us by."

During World War II, the Boeing Company established its reputation as a supplier of military aircraft. After the war, in the early fifties, Boeing made the first passenger jet, which soon replaced all of the propeller-driven aircraft in the passenger market. It has also built a number of spacecraft used in the U.S. space program. Over the years, the company has developed a strong reputation for reliable products and the service of those products. It has been number one in worldwide sales for years, controlling over 50 percent of the market for commercial aircraft.

Aerospace products are the number one U.S. export after agricultural products. The country has a long and proud tradition of dominating the industry with technological breakthroughs[1] leading to superior products. But this dominance is now being challenged.

Airbus, a France-based European company, has bumped McDonnell Douglas into the third spot in the industry, and it threatens to step up the competition. Boeing executives argue that they cannot compete against the deep pockets[2] of the four European governments that subsidize[3] Airbus. The continuing decline of the U.S. lead in aerospace has sparked an intense debate in the United States on the whole issue of the proper relationship between government and industry.

Traditionally, the United States has maintained a free-market philosophy, which holds that government should not regulate market forces. In this view, better and more efficient production occurs when world markets are open, allowing the forces of competition to work freely. According to Boeing and other executives, this philosophy has been the backbone of American industrial power from the beginning. For the health of the civil aviation industry, the free-trade argument goes, the United States must convince the EC to stop subsidizing Airbus.

However, there is less agreement than there used to be on the issue of government's role in industry and trade. Some U.S. officials and academics point out that the free-market philosophy no longer suits global economic conditions. Advocates of this emerging view urge the development of a strong industrial policy that would develop and support important U.S. industries. Such a policy could work through such protective measures as tariffs,[4] import quotas[5] or direct subsidies to industry, and through policies that encourage research in certain high-tech industries. According to this emerging view, a carefully constructed industrial policy could help the United States create jobs, increase market share, and improve profits, especially in high-tech industries.

Those in favor of the traditional free trade and open market philosophy reject the notion of an industrial policy. At worst, it sounds like the centralized planning of a socialist system. At best, it sounds like protectionism, a policy that simply uses government money to protect industries that would fail in the market without it. They point to some examples of big government-supported research projects, like the *Concorde* superfast passenger aircraft, that resulted in products that became commercial failures. Yet even the free traders have to admit that U.S. industry is not as competitive in the global economy as it once was and that, increasingly, it must compete against nations that have strong industrial policies and are unlikely to change them. So, the debate at Boeing and in the aerospace industry has far-reaching implications for the way the United States should manage its economic future.

1. significant improvements
2. unlimited wealth
3. support with government money
4. import taxes
5. limits

B. Interpreting Information

Review the information on your outline, Airbus and Boeing: A Brief Comparison. Work in small groups. Read the questions below. Discuss your answers with your classmates, and explain your opinions.

1. Airbus Industrie, a four-nation European consortium, was established in 1970 to challenge U.S. dominance in aerospace. How well has the company accomplished its goal?
2. Why do Airbus and EC officials believe subsidies for Airbus are necessary and important?
3. Why are most Boeing and U.S. officials opposed to financial backing of the airframe industry by the government?
4. If Boeing were not losing ground in the global airframe market, would it complain about Airbus subsidies?

This is the flight deck of a Boeing 747.

C. Reviewing Background Information and Vocabulary

Read the sentences and find the word or expression in the box that means the same as the italicized words. Then compare your answers with those of a classmate. If you disagree, consult another classmate, a dictionary, or your teacher.

a. aggressively seeking

b. position

c. enormous wealth

_____ 1. Since the beginning of commercial aviation, such U.S. airframe manufacturers as Boeing and McDonnell Douglas have led the industry in technological know-how and sales. Until recently, all other companies *lagged behind.*

_____ 2. Airbus Industrie was formed in 1970. For several years after, the multinational partnership was clearly *an underdog* in the airframe

d. performance history

e. a competitor that is not expected to succeed

f. developed more slowly

g. stop

h. begin to compete

i. let competitors compete on a fair and equal basis

j. feeding

industry. Boeing was not worried about the competition since nobody knew how long the new enterprise would last.

_____ 3. The Europeans hoped that Airbus would both *offset* the general decline in the airframe industry as well as challenge the dominance of U.S. companies. Even if the plan to revitalize the industry worked, they knew it would take years to reach their goal.

_____ 4. At first, Airbus had a hard time selling its planes to U.S. carriers, who buy over 50 percent of the world's aircraft. Since the products had no *track record,* airlines did not want to try them.

_____ 5. In order to *gain a foothold* in the U.S. market, Airbus offered special prices to U.S. airlines. These deals were possible because the company was subsidized by the governments of its four partners.

_____ 6. Boeing has complained about Airbus prices and the subsidies that make them possible. Officials say that no private company can compete against the *deep pockets* of four governments.

_____ 7. Airbus officials say that subsidies have helped *level the playing field* in the industry. They point out that U.S. companies get large contracts from the U.S. military. Without financial help, Airbus would not have been able to compete.

_____ 8. In just twenty years, Airbus moved into the number two *spot* in the world's airframe industry, pushing out McDonnell Douglas. This represents very rapid growth.

_____ 9. The airframe industry is expected to continue growing throughout the next decades. An increase in global business activity is *fueling* this growth.

_____10. Boeing still leads the industry with over 50 percent of the commercial market. Airbus controls about 30 percent and is *gunning for* 40 percent. The fierce competition between these two companies is certain to continue for many years.

PART 2

MAKING DECISIONS— NEGOTIATING AN INTERNATIONAL TRADE AGREEMENT

Introduction to the Problem. The commercial airframe industry is the subject of the latest round of trade talks between EC and U.S. officials. Airbus, the European consortium, and Boeing, the U.S. firm, are the two biggest competitors in the aerospace industry today. The major problem in these trade negotiations is a dispute over government subsidies.

Keep the problem in mind as you do the following exercises.

4. Exploring Business Culture: Relationships between Government and Industry

Read the information. Work in small groups to answer the questions below the chart.

Government and Industry in Three Important Regions

Japan

The Ministry of International Trade (MITI) sets a strong industrial policy.

- MITI identifies and directly supports key industries, for example, high-technology industries.
- MITI helps to gradually shut down less competitive industries.

European Community

The European Community's (EC) role in setting the industrial policies of its member nations is expanding.

- The EC had broad guidelines for development of present and future industries.
- The EC finances such long-term projects as the development of civil aircraft and high-speed trains.

United States

There is no overall industrial policy.

- The U.S. government gives research money and contracts to certain military, energy, and health industries.
- The United States has a strong free-market tradition although there is some dissatisfaction with this approach.

1. What is the relationship between government and industry in Japan, the European Community, and the United States? In which region is the relationship the closest? In which region is the relationship the most distant?

2. If you know about other regions, describe the relationship between government and industry in those regions.

3. In your view, what is the ideal relationship between government and industry?

5. Strategies for Negotiation: Identifying Areas of Agreement

A common problem for negotiators is to focus on the differences in their positions: "I want this. You want that." The negotiation easily becomes deadlocked and cannot go forward. To help overcome this problem, the participants need to identify areas of agreement. By establishing this common ground, the negotiation has a better chance of moving toward a satisfactory accord.

Here are some expressions you can use to help identify areas of agreement:

> *What seem to be our areas of agreement?*
>
> *What are your priorities? These are ours…*
>
> *We both seem to be upset about this matter. Clearly, it's important to both of us.*

1. Prepare to use the negotiating strategy. Write the expressions in the box on cards or strips of paper. Use the expressions in the exercise below.

2. Work in pairs. Student A presents the position on page 152. Student B listens, then presents the position below. Negotiate an agreement between the two neighbors. When you want to identify areas of agreement, use an expression from your cards.

Student B presents this position.

A Dispute between Neighbors
You are a concert pianist and you must practice your instrument.

*   A major recital is coming up, so you have increased your practice hours.
*   Because you work three days a week to pay the bills, you must practice at night.
*   Unless you practice with the piano lid open, you cannot hear the instrument.
*   The local law states that musical instruments can be played only between 8:00 A.M. and 11:00 P.M.

6. Conducting a Business Meeting: An International Trade Negotiation

A. Preparing for the meeting

1. **Read about the business problem.**

Airframe industry trade talks between the United States and the European Community have been dragging on for years. This latest round of talks focuses on the subsidies that Airbus receives from the governments of its four member nations. U.S. trade officials argue that open markets are better for everyone; EC officials argue that open markets do not and cannot exist. The two sides know that a trade war would be disastrous for both, so they must negotiate an accord.

2. **Notice the format of the meeting.**

Introduction
*   To open the meeting, the mediator welcomes and introduces everyone.
*   The mediator states the purpose of the talks: to negotiate an agreement on government subsidies of Airbus Industrie.

Agenda

- Each negotiating team meets to study its position and plan its strategy. The mediator moves around the room and listens in on the two teams.

- The mediator opens the negotiation, inviting participation from all delegates. When the negotiators become stuck in their positions, the mediator encourages them to identify areas of agreement in order to continue.

Closing

- The mediator summarizes the main points of agreement and disagreement.

- To close the meeting, the mediator thanks all the participants and sets a time for the next session.

3. Review your notes on the Airbus-Boeing outline, the vocabulary, the information on business culture, and the negotiating strategy of the unit. Prepare to use this information in the meeting.

B. Conducting the Meeting

Role play the trade negotiation.

- Select one person to run the negotiation as an impartial, professional mediator. He or she will begin the meeting and follow the format described above.

- Form two negotiating teams, one from the European Community and one from the United States. Read the role summaries below and on page 86. Follow the format described.

The Roles

> ### EC Trade Representatives:
> - Airbus's share of the airframe market is not yet 40 percent. Boeing's is more than 50 percent.
> - Subsidies from the governments are already down from 70 to 100 percent of product development to only about 45 percent. U.S. military contracts subsidize Boeing.
> - The EC must have a strong industrial policy (with subsidies, import taxes, and so on) to be competitive in the global market.
> - If the United States keeps control of the airframe industry, customers all over the world will be hurt. Without competition, safety and maintenance standards will decline.
> - (*Add your own.*)

U.S. Trade Representatives:

- Airbus is cutting into Boeing's market. This hurts the U.S. effort to increase exports since airplanes are the number one nonagricultural export.
- Subsidies from EC nations to Airbus allow the company to sell its airplanes too cheaply.
- If Airbus stops accepting subsidies, U.S. airframe manufacturers will also continue to refuse help from the U.S. government. The United States will maintain a free-market policy.
- If Airbus continues to accept subsidies, the U.S. government may be forced to set up such trade barriers as higher tariffs and lower import quotas.
- (*Add your own.*)

---

7. Follow-Up Activities

Negotiating International Trade Agreements

A. Business Writing

Write an interoffice letter to one of the team leaders. As a member of either the EC or the U.S. negotiating team, suggest a possible EC–U.S. trade agreement in the aircraft industry. Give reasons for your view.

For a model of an interoffice letter, see page 42.

B. Putting the Problem in Perspective: Applying Business Concepts

1. Read the summary of the business problem. Comment on the nature of the trade problem and on other international trade talks you know about.

Trade talks are extremely delicate and complex. When trading partners sit down at the negotiating table, economic, political, philosophical, and other issues are involved. The complexity of international negotiations is illustrated in the many rounds of talks involving the airframe industry.

Economics is the most obvious issue separating Airbus and Boeing. When Airbus was the underdog, *subsidies* to launch the new enterprise were not controversial. Few people, however, predicted that this *consortium* that was created to pool the resources and know-how of four European countries would so quickly be able to gain a foothold in the international airframe market and move into the number two spot in the industry. Boeing now fears that its sales may lag behind.

Any economic discussion at a trade talk, however, is closely related to both political and philosophical issues. In the United States, industry groups and unions often want to be protected from foreign competition. U.S. officials, however, come to the negotiating table with a long history of belief in the *free-market* system. In their view, open world markets benefit both producers and customers in the long run. Many U.S. policymakers are opposed to *protectionism*, whether the trade barriers take the form of *tariffs, import quotas,* or direct subsidies. In contrast, in Japan and among members of the European Community, *industrial policy* is viewed as a positive and necessary part of international competition. Industries that are important to the economy are supported. Research related to these industries is also supported. In the case of Airbus, for example, subsidies are seen as a means of leveling the playing field and helping the EC aerospace industry compete on a global scale.

Underlying any trade talks is also the issue of national pride. The success of Airbus symbolizes the hope for European cooperation and economic strength in the future. At the same time, threats to the U.S. airframe industry have always been taken as challenges to that nation's dominance in world affairs.

As a result of economic, political, philosophical, and historical differences, trade negotiations tend to drag on and on. This is true in the airframe industry. Sometimes they break down. It is rarely to anyone's advantage, however, to allow such a breakdown to escalate into a trade war.

2. Answer the questions based on what you have learned. Use the italicized expressions in your answers.

a. How might government *subsidies* help as well as hurt industry? What industries *are subsidized* in your country? Do you agree with the government's policy?

b. In the Airbus *consortium,* aerospace companies from four nations are both owners and suppliers. What advantages might such a business organization enjoy? What problems might an international high-technology *consortium* like Airbus have?

c. Why do many U.S. and Boeing officials defend a *free-market* philosophy? Why are they against creating such trade barriers as *tariffs* and *import quotas?*

d. To some nations, an *industrial policy* is essential; to many people in the United States, it sounds like *protectionism.* What is the difference? Are they always different?

e. Who are the major trading partners in your region? Are you aware of any recent changes in their trade agreements?

KIDSELEBRATION, INC.

Expanding a Small Children's Products Business

BACKGROUND

1. Examining the Products

Read the information and look at the photographs in order to become familiar with Kidselebration and some of its products. Then answer the questions.

Kidselebrati⬤n™

- Can be reached by mail at: P.O. Box 2033
  New York, NY 10113-0960
- Was founded in 1986.
- Has annual sales of $900,000.
- Has four employees and seventy-five sales representatives in the United States as well as distributors in Canada and Great Britain.

Name Tunes is a fifteen-minute personalized audiotape. The child's name is mentioned twenty-three times in its five songs. Boy's and girl's versions available. For ages birth to six years. Retail price is about seven dollars.

Here are some of the hundreds of names available for the personalized product *Name Tunes*.

Boys' Names	Girls' Names
Aaron	Hilary
Adam	Jackie
Alan	Jamie
Alex	Jasmine
Andrew	Jennifer
Angel	Jessica
Anthony	Jill
Antonio	Joanna
Austin	Julia
Benjamin	Karen
Billy	Katherine
Bobby	Kelly
Brad	Kimberly
Brandon	Kristin
Brian	Laura
Carlos	Linda
Charles	Lindsay
Christopher	Lisa

1. *Name Tunes* is an audiocassette tape for children. Why does this tape sell well in several English-speaking countries? Consider, for example, entertainment and educational value, cassette format, and price.

2. This Kidselebration product is personalized in an unusual way: The individual child's name is used many times in the songs. Have you seen this kind of product before? What do you think of it? Would such a product sell in your area? Explain.

3. Many personalized products simply use initials. What personalized items for children and adults are you familiar with? When a high-priced item is personalized, the initials are often called a monogram. Monogrammed items include silver belt buckles, crystal glassware, and custom-tailored shirts. What other monogrammed items have you seen?

2. Gathering Data: Listening

You will hear an interview with Debbie and Peter Roth, owners and creators of Kidselebration, Inc., a small children's products business. They discuss with the author what makes their products distinctive, how the business has changed their lives, and what advice they would give to others who are thinking of starting a small business. You will also hear a sample of one of their major products, *Name Tunes*, a personalized song tape for children.

A.   Read the questions. Then listen to the tape and write your answers. Compare your responses with those of a classmate. If you disagree, listen again.

1. According to Debbie and Peter Roth, the founders of Kidselebration, what is special about their company and its products?

2. Why did Peter Roth decide to start Kidselebration?

3. How has building a business affected the life-style of both Peter and Debbie Roth?

4. What advice would the Roths give to other people who might want to begin a small business?

5. There is always risk in owning a small business. How do the Roths feel about the risk now that their business has survived its first few years?

B.   Discuss your reactions to the interview with Debbie and Peter Roth. Did anything surprise or interest you particularly? What did you think of the song from *Name Tunes*? What are some things a child named Benjamin might enjoy about this song from *Name Tunes*?

3. Gathering Data: Reading

Debbie and Peter Roth, the founders of Kidselebration, have developed some winning products and created a profitable business in just a few short years. Now they are concerned with expansion.

Read these articles to gather background data on the company, including information to answer these questions:

- How did the company get started?
- What successes and difficulties has the company experienced?
- What are the challenges for the future?

A. Scanning for Information

Work in pairs. Look at Kidselebration: Brief Product History on page 93. Each person should scan one of the two articles and take notes in the appropriate section of the outline. Then, share information so that you and your partner have the same data and can fill in Kidselebration: Brief Product History completely.

1. PETER'S ORIGINAL IDEA: *NAME TUNES*

Name Tunes, the original Kidselebration product, has been a hit since it was first marketed to over 500 gift shops and specialty stores in shopping centers all over the United States.

Kidselebration founder Peter Roth cannot read music and does not play an instrument, but he is an artist when it comes to doing business. A few years ago, Peter and his wife, Debbie, were visiting musician friends with their young son, Benjamin. The friend played guitar and sang songs. When he began inserting Benjamin's name into the songs, the child lit up, becoming very excited. Suddenly the songs were not just *for* him, but they were also *about* him.

Roth had a brainstorm[1]: what if we took the idea of personalized songs and turned it into a product? Other parents and children might take to it. Tapes could be good business since they have a high profit margin, that is, they are relatively inexpensive to produce and can be sold for a good price. Peter got his friend the musician to write the songs. When he listened to the tape, he knew the lyrics and tunes were good, but the musical arrangements were not catchy[2] enough. Here is where Peter's artistry came in. He hired a professional songwriter, someone who had worked with Barbra Streisand, to rearrange the music. As Peter puts it, "I didn't want folk music, but something uplifting that would appeal to kids. When the songwriter came up with the cheerful rock 'n' roll sound, I knew it would be popular."

Name Tunes required still more work: research on names. To get lists of the most popular girls' and boys' names, Peter contacted state health departments. From these, he selected a basic list of seventy-two names.

Peter's artistry was not only to think up the product but also to create the financing to realize his idea. He borrowed $25,000 from his family and had investors put up $60,000, and he made royalty agreements with the producer of the tape (2 percent), with the songwriter (3 percent) and the singers (3 percent). "These were too generous," he admits now, "But I was inexperienced. Live and learn."

A few months later, Roth had an attorney register the fledgling[3] enterprise as a corporation in the City of New York. He also took pains to protect his ideas legally. First, he obtained legal protection for his songs, called copyright, by registering the music and lyrics[4] as the property of Kidselebration, Inc.

Then, Peter paid a professional firm to conduct a trademark search in the U.S. Trademark Office to make sure that the names of his products had not been used by anyone else. After he verified their originality, he obtained legal protections, called trademarks, for the names "Kidselebration" and "Name Tunes," as well as for the logo, the identifying symbol of the company (See the logo in the box on page 90.)

Though *Name Tunes* is protected by copyright and trademark registration, there are now seven or eight knockoffs[5] on the market. "You can protect the specific product, but you can't prevent anyone from making a personalized name tape," says Roth. Another problem is pirated tapes, which are illegal copies that are sold as originals or given to friends. Perhaps the most difficult moment in the life of the business came when Kidselebration dissolved the partnership with the musician friend who had written the original songs. He became a competitor, creating a very similar tape and undercutting Kidselebration by selling it to one of their key customers at a lower price.

Despite the problems, Peter realized that he had hit upon a potentially lucrative niche[6] in the children's product market. He was determined to make something distinctive, of high quality. *Name Tunes* was the result.

1. surprisingly good idea
2. easy to remember
3. young
4. words of a song
5. imitation products
6. place (for a particular product in a market)

Kidselebration: Brief Product History

1. Peter's Original Idea: *Name Tunes*

A. The First Idea
   1. Product idea

   2. Idea development

B. Financial Aspects
   1. Investors

   2. Royalty agreements

C. Legal Protections
   1. Copyrights for music

   2. Trademarks for names

D. Competition
   1. Outside the company

   2. Inside the company

2. More Ideas: *Name Tales, Grandma's Friend Grace,* and *Grandpa's Friend Gus*

A. Developing *Name Tales*
   1. Product idea

   2. Sales

B. A New Kind of Product: *Grace* and *Gus*
   1. The product idea and the market

   2. Reasons for failure

C. Future Challenges at Kidselebration
   1. U.S. sales

   2. International sales

2. MORE IDEAS, NAME TALES, GRANDMA'S FRIEND GRACE, GRANDPA'S FRIEND GUS

Kidselebration's first product, *Name Tunes*, was a big seller, so the Roths immediately began to work on expanding their product line. They invested $30,000 in developing *Name Tales*, a personalized story that casts the boy as a prince or the girl as a princess. Each tape contains a twenty-eight-minute adventure story in which the child's name is mentioned twenty-six times. *Name Tales*, which comes in a boys' and a girls' version, is recommended for children four to nine years old. Perhaps because it, like its predecessor *Name Tunes*, plays on[1] the personalization that is Kidselebration's distinctive feature, *Name Tales* has also sold well.

With two big sellers to their credit, Debbie and Peter Roth set out to expand sales with a slightly different product, *Grandma's Friend Grace* and *Grandpa's Friend Gus*. (See photo, p. 95) These are doll and tape packages, costing about twice the price of *Name Tunes* and *Name Tales*, that target the grandparent market. What gift can you send when you are far away from your grandchildren? A good pos-

sibility is to send a friend with a tape that talks and sings about the special feelings grandparents have for their grandchildren.

The soft dolls are twelve inches high and depict a friendly older man, Gus, or older woman, Grace, people who could be friends of a child's grandparents. The tape that accompanies each doll has twenty-five minutes of original songs interspersed with stories about grandparents and grandchildren. The *Grandma's Friend Grace* tape begins with a short explanation: "Hi, my name is Grace, and I'm a friend of your Grandma. She sent me to become your friend, too. And to sing and tell stories and play games and do all the things your Grandma would do if she were here."

Like grandparents in many places, U.S. grandparents are always on the lookout for nice gifts for their grandchildren. Those with discretionary income[2] would like a unique product, so the grandparent market is a good one to tap.[3]

Or so figured Peter and Debbie Roth. They tried the idea out on friends and friends' children. They went through the copyright process again, obtaining legal protection for the product name and the identifying company symbol, the logo. (See the Kidselebration logo in the box, p. 90.) They made the company's first overseas manufacturing deal, arranging to have the first 12,000 dolls made in China. They took early examples, or prototypes, to trade shows. Everybody seemed enthusiastic about Grace and Gus. But the products have been on the shelves for about

a year now, and not enough have sold.

"Every new product is a risk," says Debbie Roth, "but we really thought we had a winner here. Why didn't Grace and Gus sell? I think, in the end, it had to do with the complexity of the concept. You can't explain this product in a phrase. It takes a few sentences. This is a doll and a tape. The doll represents a friend of the grandparent, not the grandparent." There was another issue too: What do grandparents and their friends look like? "Aging is a sensitive issue in the United States. Nobody wants to look old," remarks Debbie. "And Grace was too old-fashioned for some people."

The Roths are disappointed that the Grace and Gus products failed to sell, but they have come to accept the setbacks of business ownership. Another challenge they are facing is how to respond to a nationwide decrease in the number of independently owned high-end[4] gift stores. Chain stores, specializing in high-volume and low-price sales, are eating into the business, which translates into declining sales for Kidselebration. Meanwhile, the original ideas, *Name Tunes* and *Name Tales*, are starting to sell in Canada and Great Britain, and the Roths have made some contacts in Australia and New Zealand. Kidselebration is a going concern.[5]

---

1. makes good use of
2. money to spend (after basic needs are paid for)
3. make money from
4. expensive and high-quality
5. profit-making business

B. Interpreting Information

Review the information in your Kidselebration: Brief Product History outline. Read the questions below. Discuss your answers and explain your opinions.

1. Why are the tapes *Name Tunes* and *Name Tales* so successful?
2. Look at the photograph of *Grandpa's Friend Gus* and *Grandma's Friend Grace*. Consider what the Roths said about problems with these products. Why do you think these tape and doll products have failed to sell?

Grandma's Friend Grace and *Grandpa's Friend Gus* are tape and doll products. The twelve-inch doll represents a friend of the child's grandmother or grandfather. This friend sings songs to the child. Each tape has twenty-five minutes of songs and stories about grandparents and grandchildren.

The first song on the *Grace* tape begins:
"Grandma's friend, Grandma's friend, let's pretend that Grandma's near.
Grandma's friend, Grandma's friend, makes it clear that Grandma's love is here."

C. Reviewing Background Information and Vocabulary

Read the sentences and find the word or expression in the box that means the same as the italicized words. Then compare your answers with those of a classmate. If you disagree, consult another classmate, a dictionary, or your teacher.

a. balancing

b. surprisingly good idea

c. searching

d. unclear issues

e. worked carefully

f. suddenly thought of

_____ 1. When Peter Roth saw his child's excited reaction to a song with his own name in it, he *figured* he could turn this idea into a successful product. The project would require money and creativity, but he thought it would succeed.

_____ 2. It takes more than a *brainstorm* to build a successful business, however. Roth knew he had an imaginative idea, but he also had to obtain financing for the enterprise and legal protection for his product plans. It would take a great deal of work.

_____ 3. Roth *took pains* to develop a high-quality product. He insisted on getting catchy musical arrangements and on having the songs produced by a professional recording studio.

g. make good use of

h. disappointments

i. believed

j. intended for

_____ 4. After the success of Name Tunes, his first children's product, Roth was *on the lookout* for another idea to expand the business.

_____ 5. After considering many possibilities, he and his wife *hit upon* the idea of a personalized name story. It would be an adventure, the child would be the hero, and the child's name would be used many times throughout the story. They decided to call it Name Tales.

_____ 6. Name Tales is *geared to* slightly older children than Name Tunes. The children have to be able to follow the story and listen for almost thirty minutes.

_____ 7. Kidselebration has had a lot of success with Name Tunes and Name Tales, but the company has had *setbacks*, too. One of the more difficult experiences was the failure of the tape and doll packages called Grandpa's Friend Gus and Grandma's Friend Grace.

_____ 8. Perhaps the Grace and Gus products failed because they did not *play on* Kidselebration's most distinctive product feature: using a child's name over and over in a song or story.

_____ 9. Debbie Roth says that *juggling* work and home life is a big challenge in running the business. She has to find time to be a mother as well as a vice president.

_____ 10. As an entrepreneur, Peter Roth says that some of the business issues you have to deal with are clear, but there are a lot of *gray areas*, too.

PART 2

MAKING DECISIONS— EXPANDING A SMALL CHILDREN'S PRODUCTS BUSINESS

Introduction to the Problem. Kidselebration was doing well, but the failure of the new Grace and Gus products has been a significant setback. The company needs to continue growing in order to remain healthy. This time, however, the Roths want to study a number of options before choosing the best way to expand their business. What new products and markets should they explore?

Keep the question in mind as you do the following exercises.

4. Exploring Business Culture: Copyrights and Trademarks

Read the information. Work in small groups to answer the questions.

Copyrights and trademarks are two common forms of legal protection for intellectual property that are available to businesses and individuals in most countries. A copyright gives the legal right to be the only producer or seller of a song, book, movie, and so on for a fixed period of time. Before offering *Name Tunes* for sale, for example, the Roths copyrighted the music and lyrics. In the United States, a copyright is granted for twenty-eight years, with the possibility of renewal for another twenty-eight years. Copyrighted material often has a statement or a small *c* on the product or packaging to identify it. Material without copyright is in the public domain and can be reproduced without permission.

Trademarks are used to help companies establish and keep their own identities. The Roths, for example, trademarked both the name "Kidselebration" and the company symbol, or logo, as marks that identify their products. [The logo appears on page 90.] In the United States, trademarks are often accompanied by the letter *R* or *TM*, meaning Registered Trademark, in a small circle next to the registered name or symbol.

In many countries, if your copyrighted or trademarked material is used without permission, you can bring your case to a court of law. There are penalties and fines for infringement of these legal guarantees of ownership.

Copyright protections are guaranteed internationally by multilateral treaties. The most important of these is the Berne Convention, created in 1886. Up until now, seventy-seven nations, with the notable exceptions of the People's Republic of China and the states of the former Soviet Union, have signed the treaty. These nations agree to recognize copyright protection across their national boundaries. In the words of the treaty, this means that "authors should enjoy in other countries the same protection for their works as those countries accord to their own authors."

1. What is the main difference between a copyright and a trademark? Why do the owners of Kidselebration need both kinds of legal protections for their intellectual property?

2. What is the importance of the Berne Convention? What problems might there be with such a treaty? What problems might there be without such a treaty?

3. Have you seen examples of infringement of international copyrights or trademarks? What illegal reproductions of products have you seen? What can be done about this problem?

5. Strategies for Negotiation: Eliciting More Information

Eliciting information is a strategy managers can use to get people to expand on their ideas. Sometimes the kernel of an idea can be developed through discussion into something very useful for business. Also, eliciting information is a useful way to help understand another person's point of view, priorities, and concerns.

Here are some expressions you can use to elicit more information:

> *I'd like to know more about that.*
>
> *Could you explain what you mean by...?*
>
> *Really? That's interesting. What exactly do you have in mind?*

1. **Prepare to use the negotiating strategy. Write the phrases for eliciting more information on cards or strips of paper. Use these expressions in the exercise.**

2. **Work in pairs. Student A has information about Idea 1; Student B should not look at this information. Student A gives the information about Idea 1 to Student B, one piece at a time. Student B elicits each piece of information, using expressions from the cards. Finally, discuss your opinion of the business idea.**

Then, Student B gives information about Idea 2 on page 153 to Student A, one piece at a time. Student A elicits each piece of information, using expressions from the cards. Again, discuss your opinion of the business idea.

Student A uses this information.

Idea 1. You work for Kidselebration. Your idea is to work with a manufacturer of tape players. Kidselebration advertising could be included with each tape player. Try to get your partner interested in this idea by revealing one detail at a time.

- My idea is that we could contact tape recorder manufacturers.
- Next, we would make a deal with the manufacturers.
- The deal could be an exchange: They can use part of a *Name Tunes* song to advertise cassette recorders on the radio.
- In exchange, we would be able to place discount coupons for Kidselebration products inside of the packaging of their tape recorders. Consumers would send in the coupons.
- Then, we would send the tape and add their name and address to our mailing list. What do you think of the idea? Can it work?

6. Conducting a Business Meeting: A Meeting with Consultants

A. Preparing for the Meeting

1. **Read about the business problem.**

> Kidselebration, Inc., is a small business whose owners have carved out a special niche in the children's market: personalized name tunes and stories. The company's mission is to create fun products that help children develop self-esteem. After a successful start-up, the business is at a crossroads. Its sales are down and its newest products, *Grandma's Friend Grace* and *Grandpa's Friend Gus*, have failed to sell. At this meeting, Kidselebration owners Debbie and Peter Roth hope the consultants will come up with good ideas for expanding the business.

2. **Notice the format of the meeting.**

Introduction
- Vice President Debbie Roth (VP) opens the meeting by welcoming and introducing everyone.
- She states the purpose of the meeting: to generate at least three concrete proposals to expand Kidselebration and increase its sales.

Agenda
- Three task forces from the same consulting firm work independently to brainstorm specific proposals for Kidselebration. Debbie Roth moves around the room and listens in on the groups.
- Each task force makes a brief presentation of its proposal to the whole class. When appropriate, the VP elicits more detailed information from participants.

Closing
- Roth closes the meeting by thanking everyone. She says she will decide on which proposal to implement first within five business days.

3. **Review your notes on Kidselebration's Brief Product History outline, the vocabulary, the information on business culture, and the negotiating strategy of the unit. Prepare to use this information in the meeting.**

B. Conducting the Meeting

Role play the meeting with consultants.

- Select one person to run the meeting as Debbie Roth, vice president of Kidselebration, Inc. Ms. Roth will begin the meeting and follow the format described.
- Form three task forces, all from the same consulting company. Read the role summaries on page 100. Follow the meeting format described.

The Roles

Task Force on Developing New Tape Products

Your group will propose a new tape product that helps children develop self-esteem. Discuss these questions to help generate ideas:

- What about tapping the grandparent market with a personalized tape product?
- What about creating tapes for holidays or special events in a child's life?
- What about tape products for teenagers?

Task Force on Internationalizing Existing Products

Your group will consider translating the personalized tunes and tales into other languages. Use these questions to get ideas:

- What languages would have the largest market for Kidselebration products? Why?
- What accent or variety of the languages should be used? Why?
- Which names should be used for personalization?

Task Force on Exploring New Sales Strategies

Your idea is to boost sales of *Name Tunes* and *Name Tales* by proposing new sales strategies. Now, seventy-five sales representatives sell Kidselebration products to 500 high-end gift stores. Discuss these questions to help generate ideas:

- How could Kidselebration get media attention without paying for advertising?
- Should the products be available in large discount stores?
- How could the grandparent market be reached more effectively?

---

7. Follow-Up Activities

A. Business Writing

Choose one of the following topics.

1. As Debbie or Peter Roth, write a letter to a potential investor, or venture capitalist, with your plans for expanding Kidselebration, your successful small business. Describe the plans for expansion (based on the discussion in Exercise 6) and the amount of money you believe these plans will require. Give reasons why this would be a good business opportunity for the investor. For a model of a business letter, see page 28.

2. Imagine that you are an entrepreneur with a good business idea. Write to a potential investor, or venture capitalist, with your business plan. Describe the product or service and the amount of money your plan will require. Give reasons why this would be a good business opportunity for the investor. For a model of a business letter, see page 28.

B. Putting the Problem in Perspective: Applying Business Concepts

1. Read this summary of the business problem. Comment on the quality of the Roth's business decisions.

Starting a Small Business

Would you like to start a small business? As entrepreneurs Debbie and Peter Roth of Kidselebration can tell you, turning a *fledgling enterprise* into a going concern requires a willingness to live with risk, overcome setbacks, and work hard. But there are big rewards, too. You can take control of your life and increase your family's assets.

If you want to start a business, there are a number of questions to consider. What will your *mission* be? According to Peter Roth, it should be something you believe in passionately. As parents and business partners, the Roths' mission was clear: to design quality products to develop children's self-esteem.

What will your product be? Competition is fierce. It seems that as soon as you have created an original product for a new *market niche*, a competitor appears with a *knockoff*, an imitation of your product that can seriously *undercut* your business. One way to protect your intellectual property is to apply for *copyrights* and *trademarks*. For the Roths, this strategy prevented *copyright infringement*, but it did not prevent a number of knockoffs. Another strategy is to create a product with a high *profit margin*, something that can be sold at several times the manufacturing price. The Roths found that cassette tapes have a high profit margin.

Which market will you try to *tap*? You have to consider which segments of the population have *discretionary income* to spend on your product or service. The Roths have found that adults will buy Kidselebration products because they figure these tapes are both fun and good for children.

How will your *life-style* can be affected by business ownership? The Roths find they have to work harder, but they can choose their own hours. For Debbie Roth, this flexibility is essential in juggling her roles as mother and businesswoman.

What does it take to create a successful small business? Most entrepreneurs agree that you have to believe in yourself and be able to recover from failure. Roth adds that the risk changes, but it does not disappear. No longer worried about survival, his new concern is maintaining the quality of future Kidselebration products.

2. **Answer the questions based on what you have learned. Use the italicized expressions in your answers.**

a. Imagine yourself as an entrepreneur, a creator of a small business. What product or service would your *fledgling enterprise* choose to sell? What would your *mission* be? Which market would you try to *tap*? How could your product or service be geared to people who have the *discretionary income* to buy it?

b. Successful products often create their own *market niche*, defining or expanding a product category. What *market niche* has Kidselebration created?

c. *Knockoffs* of consumer products can *undercut* a business. How have the Roths used *copyrights* and *trademarks* to protect their property? What protections would be available for their products in your area? Is *copyright infringement* a problem?

d. *Profit margins* in cassettes are high. For example, it might cost fifty cents to copy a cassette. You could sell it wholesale to a distributor for $3.95, and the retailer, in turn, could charge the customer $6.95. Why is the *profit margin* so high?

e. Running a small business affects your *life-style*. The Roths enjoy being responsible for their own time and money. In what ways would your *life-style* be affected if you created your own business?

C. Fieldwork

Report to the class on a successful small business in the area.

- Gather data by interviewing the owner.
- Look at the questions in Exercise 2. You may want to use them as an interview guide.

AKZO N.V.

Responding to Environmental Concerns in Europe

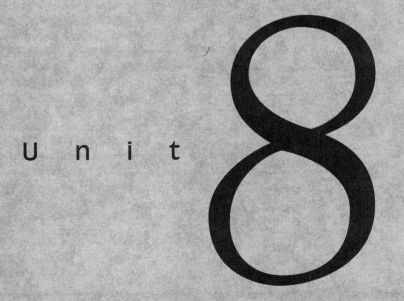

Unit 8

PART 1

BACKGROUND

1. Examining the Products

Read the information and look at the photographs in order to become familiar with Akzo and some of its products. Then answer the questions.

Akzo n.v.

- Has its headquarters at Velperweg 76
  P.O. Box 9300
  6800 SB Arnhem
  The Netherlands.
- Was established in 1969.
- Has sales of 16,851 millions of Dutch guilders (U.S. $9.1 billion).
- Is a worldwide group of companies operating in fifty countries in several regions, including Europe, North America, and Asia.

Among Akzo's products are paints and fibers used for many purposes.

---

1. Akzo produces chemicals, fibers, paints, and healthcare products. Should this company be concerned about the environment? Why, or why not?
2. Are you concerned about the environment? The environmental, or "green," movement urges individuals to reduce, reuse, and recycle the products that they use. How can you help?
3. Environmentalists tell us to "think globally, and act locally." What does this phrase mean? Do you think this idea is important? Why, or why not?

2. Gathering Data: Listening

You will hear an interview with John Behan, a specialist in environmental law and a lawyer for Akzo America, Inc. He discusses with the author Akzo's environmental policies and some major concepts in environmental regulation.

A.   Read the questions. Then listen to the tape and write your answers. Compare your responses with those of a classmate. If you disagree, listen again.

1. According to Mr. Behan, what is distinctive about Akzo?

_____

_____

2. When did U.S. businesses first become aware of environmental concerns? When did European Community (EC) businesses become aware? When did Akzo become aware, and why?

_____

_____

3. Economic development and environmental protection may seem incompatible, so government and business leaders now refer to "sustainable business development" as a goal. What does this concept mean?

_____

_____

4. "Strict liability" is a major theme in environmental regulation. What does this concept mean to businesses like Akzo?

_____

_____

5. Each business unit manager at Akzo is responsible for complying with the company's environmental policy. In what two ways does Akzo encourage unit managers to be environmentally responsible?

_____

_____

B.   Discuss your reaction to the interview with John Behan. Did anything surprise or interest you particularly? What do you think of his way of doing business?

3. Gathering Data: Reading

Akzo, a Dutch-owned multinational chemical corporation, takes responsibility for the environmental impact of its products. Recently, Akzo has had to respond to environmental concerns about chlorine.

Read the articles to gather background data on the company's activities in this area, including information to answer these questions:

- How has Akzo's environmental policy evolved?
- What are the problems and risks associated with chlorine?
- How is Akzo managing the chlorine issue?

Work in pairs. Look at the outline called Akzo and the Environment on page 107. Each person should scan one of the articles and take notes in the appropriate section of the outline. Then, share information so that you and your partner have the same data and can fill in the Akzo and the Environment outline completely.

1. AKZO BECOMES A "CLEAN COMPANY"

Akzo n.v. is the world's largest producer of salt, the second-largest producer of paint, and one of the largest producers of man-made fibers. It is the Netherlands' largest producer of chlorine (Cl), an element occurring naturally in salt (NaCl). This diversified chemical company was formed in 1969 through the merger of two Dutch companies with very different markets, Algemene Kunstzijde Unie (AKU) and Koninklijke Zout Organon (KZO). The *n.v.* in Akzo's name stands for *naamloze vennootschap*, which means nameless partnership. It now operates in fifty countries and employs over 60,000 people worldwide.

In 1989, twenty years after its establishment, Akzo senior executives decided to reorganize the company into four product groups: fibers, chemicals, paints, and health care. Each of these groups includes a number of business units that function as semi-independent research and financial departments. Akzo executives believe that the decentralized business-unit structure gives the company more flexibility to respond to the market. Environmental policy is made by the highest company officials, but it is the responsibility of each business unit to apply the corporate environmental and safety standards to its own industrial sites.

As a chemical company, Akzo must be concerned with environmental protection because many of its processes and products can pollute air, water, and soil if they are not managed carefully. Akzo's environmental policy has developed along with the growing amount of government regulation of industry. At first, the company, like many others, reacted to new environmental laws by implementing end-of-pipe solutions, that is, by making environmentally unsafe material leftover at the end of the manufacturing process, or industrial waste, less harmful through a treatment process. In the early days of environmental awareness and government regulation, these efforts were considered an adequate response.

In the next stage in the evolution of Akzo's environmental policy, the company has focused on reducing or preventing pollution by developing environmental management systems (EMS). The purpose is to make environmental concerns part of industrial operations and management from the start of each project. Instead of treating industrial waste after it is produced by a manufacturing process, these systems aim to reduce the amount of waste that is produced from the beginning. To comply with[1] the environmental management system, Akzo employees at each manufacturing site must make sure that everything possible is done to reduce harmful waste and reduce the use of nonrenewable resources.[2] With EMS, the environmental aspect of manufacturing is viewed as an essential part of the operation.

To make sure that the environmental management system of each site is functioning properly, Akzo has instituted regular health, safety, and environmental (HSE) audits.[3] Small groups of Akzo and outside experts visit Akzo plants to identify problems and check for compliance with Akzo's as well as local and national regulations. After an HSE audit, a site receives a rating of good, acceptable with recommendations, or to be improved. Akzo points out that these check-up mechanisms are more demanding than the voluntary ecology audits recommended by the European Community Council of Environmental Ministers.

So, Akzo has moved quickly from reactive end-of-pipe solutions to proactive environmental management systems that anticipate and prevent problems. Recently the focus of Akzo's environmental policy has become the management of product life cycles. This means that the company is concerned with the entire life of a product, from the raw materials that go into making it, to the waste from the process that manufactures it, and, finally, to its disposal after customers use the product.

As a chemical company, Akzo will continue to be under fire[4] from environmentalists and government officials for many years to come. Its current policies comply with the Dutch National Environmental Policy Plan, a comprehensive set of over 200 laws, but regulation will increase and responding to environmental concerns will continue to require a great deal of time and money. At the same time, the development of safer and cleaner manufacturing processes and products can offer business opportunities. Executives at Akzo believe that it must operate as a "clean company" or a "sustainable business" that cleans up as it manufactures. Only in this way will Akzo be able to survive and prosper in the future.

1. obey (rules or laws)
2. energy sources such as coal and oil that cannot be replaced
3. official reviews
4. be criticized

Akzo and the Environment

1. Akzo Becomes a "Clean Company"

A. Company Structure
   1. Merger

   2. Reorganization

   3. Responsibility for environmental policy

B. Evolution of Environmental Policy
   1. End-of-pipe solutions

   2. Environmental management systems

   3. Product life cycle management

   4. Dutch national environmental policy

2. An Environmental Concern for Akzo: Chlorine

A. Importance of Chlorine
   1. Importance to Akzo

   2. Importance to modern life

B. Problems with Chlorine
   1. Production

   2. Transportation

   3. Disposal

C. Life Cycle Management of Chlorine
   1. Reduce, Reuse, Recycle

   2. Proximity of producers and users

2. AN ENVIRONMENTAL CONCERN FOR AKZO: CHLORINE

Akzo n.v. is the world's largest producer of salt, the second-largest producer of paint, and one of the largest producers of man-made fibers. It is the largest producer of chlorine in the Netherlands. This diversified corporation was formed in 1969 through the merger of two Dutch companies with very different markets, Algemene Kunstzijde Unie (AKU) and Koninklijke Zout Organon (KZO). The *n.v.* in Akzo's name stands for *naamloze vennootschap,* which means nameless partnership. It now operates in fifty countries and employs over 60,000 people worldwide.

As a chemical company, Akzo must be concerned about the potential risks to the environment of creating, using, and transporting its products. The management of chlorine is of special interest to Akzo. It is one of the company's major products. Chlorine occurs in nature as a gas, but it is transported as a liquid. In both forms, it is extremely hazardous.[1] The management of chlorine and chlorine-derived products is a good example of how Akzo responds to environmental concerns.

Chlorine (Cl), which is an element that occurs naturally in salt (NaCl), is essential to modern life. Without it, we would not enjoy the same standard of living. Because it combines with nearly all other elements, chlorine has many uses. It is used widely to purify water for drinking and as a bleaching and cleaning agent. Chlorine is also a key ingredient in the manufacture of plastics, glass, clothing, and cars.

At its three Dutch plants, at Rotterdam, Delfzijl, and Hengelo, Akzo produces 460,000 metric tons of chlorine annually. The company is keenly aware of the hazards associated with its production, transportation, and disposal, and works constantly to reduce these risks.

Emissions from the chlorine production process are a problem because chlorine gas is highly irritating and volatile.[2] Over the past few years, however, Akzo has invested in new constructions at its three plants that have considerably reduced emissions of harmful substances. In addition, Akzo scientists developed a process for chlorine production that is cleaner and safer than the other common processes. This environmentally friendly technology, called the membrane process, is used at Akzo's Rotterdam plant.

In addition to environmental problems in chlorine production, there are serious risks in chlorine transportation. Liquid chlorine is so volatile that, in the Netherlands, it can be transported only in trains consisting of special railroad cars. To minimize the risk of explosion or accident, these trains move at night, at a maximum speed of 65 kph (40.3 mph), with constant supervision. These regulations reduce the risks associated with the transport of chlorine, but such risks cannot be eliminated completely.

The third major issue related to chlorine is the disposal of certain types of chlorine waste. For example, plastics made with chlorine, called PVC or polyvinyl chloride, fill city garbage dumps with toys, floor coverings, and other plastic-based products. These plastics must be collected and recycled. Chlorine waste is also a problem in the drycleaning process. The chlorine-containing solvents[3] used to clean clothing are emitted into the air, and are usually not recycled. The disposal of plastics and drycleaning solvents are only two of the difficult problems associated with waste from chlorine-containing products.

It is Akzo's goal to manage the entire life cycle of chlorine so that environmental and safety risks are minimized. This means that the company is concerned with the whole life of chlorine, from the raw materials that go into producing it, to the waste from manufacturing processes and, finally, to disposal of chlorine-containing products after customers have used them. As steps toward this goal, Akzo has already developed processes that reduce emissions during manufacturing. It is working to perfect recycling and reuse processes for chlorine so that wastes would be reincorporated into future manufacturing processes and, in effect, would no longer be waste. In addition, it is trying to locate facilities for production and usage of chlorine as geographically close to each other as possible, an idea known as the proximity principle, to reduce safety and environmental risks. With life-cycle management in place, chlorine production should have little negative impact on the environment.

1. dangerous

2. causes severe discomfort to skin and eyes and is explosive

3. liquids that can dissolve other substances

B. Interpreting Information

Review the information in your outline, Akzo and the Environment, on page 107. Read the questions below. Working in small groups, discuss your answers. Explain your opinions.

1. How have Akzo's corporate environmental policies changed the way the company conducts its business?
2. a. What are the advantages and disadvantages of chlorine as a product?
   b. What are the advantages and disadvantages of Akzo's approach to chlorine production and management?
3. Look at the pie chart below. What percentage of the Netherlands' total chlorine production comes from Akzo's three plants? How large is the production of Akzo's Rotterdam plant compared to that of its other two plants? Why is this important?

A 38% Akzo Rotterdam
B 29% Overig (niet Akzo)
C 22% Akzo Delfzijl
D 11% Akzo Hengelo

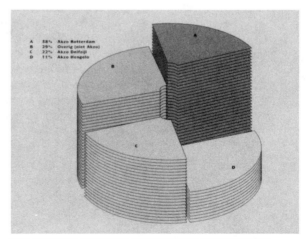

This is a three-dimensional pie chart showing chlorine capacity in the Netherlands, which totals 650,000 tons.

C. Reviewing Background Information and Vocabulary

Read the sentences and find the word or expression in the box that means the same as the italicized words. Then compare your answers with those of a classmate. If you disagree, consult another classmate, a dictionary, or your teacher.

a. officially reviewed

b. be criticized

c. joined together

d. dangerous

e. throw out

f. released

g. anticipates needs

h. established

i. rules and procedures

j. be better prepared than is required

k. put in danger

_____ 1. To form Akzo n.v., two existing companies *merged*. The two businesses together have more resources and expertise than either one alone.

_____ 2. To respond more quickly to the market, Akzo has reorganized itself into business units. In this way, it hopes to reduce the *red tape* that can prevent a new idea from becoming a new product quickly.

_____ 3. Environmentalists watch industry carefully. Akzo is aware that its operations may *be under fire* from these groups in the future.

_____ 4. Akzo does not simply wait for the government to establish regulations. Rather, it *is proactive* and sets its own higher standards for environmental protection.

_____ 5. Akzo has *instituted* an advanced protection plan called an environmental management system (EMS). Each manufacturing site has an individualized plan.

_____ 6. Akzo's idea in environmental regulation is not simply to follow the law, but to *be ahead of the game*. According to top executives, this makes Akzo more competitive.

_____ 7. At its industrial plants, Akzo aims to reduce waste that is *emitted* into the soil, air, and water.

_____ 8. Another of Akzo's concerns is the management of *hazardous* waste. This material may be a threat to the environment or to public safety.

_____ 9. It is necessary to *dispose of* chemicals carefully. They cannot be treated like ordinary garbage. Akzo spends a lot of money to manage chemical waste responsibly.

_____10. In Akzo's environmental plan, its industrial sites are *audited* regularly. Experts come to see whether the operations are as "green" and "clean" as company policy requires.

_____11. Environmental policy is a complex matter for business. Companies do not want to *jeopardize* the environment or their profits, so policies have to balance these interests.

MAKING DECISIONS—RESPONDING TO ENVIRONMENTAL CONCERNS

Introduction to the Problem. The impact of environmental concerns on business in Europe and elsewhere is increasing. Akzo has a strong environmental policy, but it also has an interest in expanding. The company is seeking permission to increase its chlorine capacity at the Rotterdam plant. The problem is that Akzo has run into some serious opposition from environmentalists.

Keep the problem in mind as you do the following exercises.

4. Exploring Business Culture: Environmentally Safe Manufacturing

Read the information. Work in small groups to answer the questions.

Effective environmental management is now a very important part of manufacturing in many countries.

The Netherlands, where Akzo is headquartered, is one of the most environmentally concerned nations in the European Community. The Dutch National Policy Plan, known as NMP Plus, is a comprehensive set of more than 200 environmental laws. It includes regulations for noise, water, soil, and air pollution as well as measures relating specifically to disposal of hazardous waste. In general, the laws aim to reduce or prevent pollution by making it much cheaper and more effective for industry to be "green" from the start than to clean up environmental damage afterwards.

Before constructing or operating a new manufacturing plant in the Netherlands, local and foreign businesses must obtain licenses and inform the Dutch authorities about the details of their plans. The process typically lasts about seven months. In this way, the Dutch government assures itself that the operation is in compliance with NMP Plus and thus will be safe and clean for the environment. Failure to comply can result in expensive legal claims and delays.

Akzo's environmental management system (EMS) was designed not only to comply with Dutch law but also to avoid future problems. It seems clear that the European Community Council of Environmental Ministers will increase the number and strength of its "green" objectives. As agreed, these must then be translated into law in each member nation. It is clear to Akzo that companies with energetic, proactive approaches to environmental protection and safety will be more likely to do better. These "clean" companies will be able to satisfy national and international regulators, avoid legal claims for environmentally unsafe practices and the bad publicity they bring, and still make a healthy profit.

1. What is the purpose of the Dutch National Environmental Policy (NMP Plus)?
2. If you want to construct and operate a large manufacturing plant in the Netherlands, how does NMP Plus affect you?
3. Why does Akzo want to have higher standards of environmental protection than the current Dutch government requires?
4. Is there an environmental or "green" movement in your area? Are there environmental laws? Can you give an example of how industry is affected?

5. Strategies for Negotiation: Interrupting for Clarification

Interrupting for clarification is a strategy that international business managers need in order to compensate for such common obstacles to communication as fatigue, noise, a speaker's pronunciation, or one's own listening skills. As a participant in a negotiation or meeting of any kind, it is your responsibility to interrupt politely a speaker whom you cannot understand or cannot hear.

Here are some expressions you can use to interrupt for clarification:

I'm sorry. I $\begin{Bmatrix} didn't \\ couldn't \end{Bmatrix}$ *catch what you said. Could you say it again, please?*

Excuse me. I $\begin{Bmatrix} didn't \\ couldn't \end{Bmatrix}$ *hear what you said. Would you mind repeating it?*

1.   **Prepare to use the negotiating strategy. Write the phrases for interrupting for clarification on cards or strips of paper. Use these expressions in the exercise.**

2.   **Work in pairs. Student A will work with Issue 1. Student A reads the information about Issue 1 to Student B. Student B listens carefully. Student B should not look at Issue 1. The information contains some nonsense words. When Student B needs clarification, he or she interrupts Student A, using expressions from the cards. When Student A repeats the sentence, he or she substitutes meaningful words for the nonsense words. These meaningful words are found in the footnotes.**

Then, switch roles. Student B works with Issue 2 on page 153, the same procedure. Finally, discuss both issues.

Student A reads this information.

Issue 1: Cleaning Up Hazardous Waste

   Who should clean up hazardous waste? This is a difficult environmental issue. Some people argue that the <u>badada</u>[1] should pay for the clean-up. This is called the "polluter-pays" principle. There are some problems with this idea, however. One problem is that sometimes the polluter is unknown or out of business. Another problem is that clean-up is very expensive and may even be impossible with current <u>doodle</u>.[2] Other people argue that some public funds must be spent. The job is too big and too expensive for private companies. They will not be able to clean the sites well enough.

   The European Community Council of Environmental Ministers favors a high tax on new hazardous waste. Nevertheless, nobody seems to have a good answer for what to do with <u>malala</u>.[3] The council is trying to establish some guidelines.

1. polluter
2. technology
3. old waste

6. Conducting a Business Meeting: A Public Meeting

A. Preparing for the Meeting

1. Read about the business problem.

Akzo, the largest chlorine producer in the Netherlands, has applied for permission to expand its chlorine plant in the city of Rotterdam. The company has complied with all environmental regulations, but many people are against the proposed expansion. Chlorine and its wastes can be hazardous to the environment and to public safety. At this public meeting, Akzo executives try to convince the Dutch Environmental Ministry and the Dutch public that, despite some risks, there are important benefits to their proposed chlorine plant expansion.

2. Notice the format of the meeting.

Introduction

- The mayor of Rotterdam opens the meeting by welcoming and introducing everyone.
- The mayor states the purpose of the meeting: to discuss whether Akzo should be granted permission to expand its Rotterdam chlorine plant, and under what conditions.

Agenda

- Each group meets to discuss the problem. The mayor moves around the room and listens in on the groups.
- The mayor invites all participants to discuss the potential risks and benefits of Akzo's plant expansion. When appropriate, participants interrupt each other for clarification.

Closing

- The mayor summarizes the main risks and benefits discussed. If an agreement is reached, the mayor states whether permission will be granted and under what conditions. If there is no agreement, the mayor calls another meeting.

3. Review your notes on the Akzo and the Environment outline, the vocabulary, the information on business culture, and the negotiating strategy in the unit. Prepare to use this information in the meeting.

B. Conducting the Meeting

Role play the public meeting.

- Select one person to run the meeting as the mayor of Rotterdam. He or she will begin the meeting and follow the format described above.
- Form three groups: Akzo executives, Dutch Environmental Ministry officials, and Dutch Citizens Concerned about the Environment. Read the role summaries below and on page 115. These groups will follow the meeting format described.

The Roles

Akzo Executives

You want permission to expand the chlorine production facility in Rotterdam from 240,000 to 250,000 metric tons annually. This increase will benefit your business and the country.

- This plant expansion will reduce environmental risk by:

  eliminating chlorine rail transports to Rotterdam from Akzo's other two plants.

  increasing Akzo's use of its cleaner and safer chlorine production process.

- Akzo helps the country by providing over 3,500 jobs and by promoting Dutch business.

- Akzo is investing 55.5 million guilders (U.S. $30 million) in research to make chlorine safer for the environment in the future.

- *(Add your own.)*

Dutch Environmental Ministry Officials

You want to weigh the risk and benefits of Akzo's proposed chlorine plant expansion. Your goal is to promote environmentally safe development.

- Akzo must comply with all of the regulations in the Dutch government's NMP Plus plan, and file a detailed report of the company's plans.

- Akzo should show how this expansion is part of life-cycle management of chlorine.

- Akzo should show that a 10,000-ton increase is safe and necessary.

- *(Add your own.)*

7. Follow-Up Activities

A. Business Writing

Write a business letter. As a Dutch official, write to a senior executive at Akzo. Respond to his or her letter requesting a license to expand Akzo's chlorine capacity at its Rotterdam plant.

For a model of a business letter, see page 28.

B. Putting the Problem in Perspective: Applying Business Concepts

1. Read the summary. Comment on the quality of Akzo's business decisions.

Responding to Environmental Concerns

Not long ago, protecting the environment was the concern of a small group of people on the radical edge of society. Now, the environment is at the center of public debate. And as Akzo's experience shows, environmental concerns can have a very large impact on business.

Compliance with environmental regulations is a major concern of any manufacturing company. The number and strictness of regulations on the national and international level will continue to grow. Akzo, for example, must comply with Dutch law, but it also must follow regulatory trends in the European Community. So far, the law in both cases considers the polluter *strictly liable* for air pollution, soil contamination, and hazardous waste disposal. If manufacturing operations pollute, the business must pay for *environmental clean-up*. In addition, it must pay a fine, which can be a large sum of money.

Many businesses discover that simply reacting to regulations is not cost-effective. They do better to invest in significant changes in their operations. Akzo, for example, realized that *end-of-pipe solutions*, treatments of chemical waste, would not be adequate for environmental protection. Instead, it would make more business sense to reduce the amount of waste and recycle any waste that was produced. Ideally, the company would take "cradle-to-grave" responsibility for all materials it uses or produces. It would see that the chemicals were handled responsibly at every stage, from raw material through final disposal. These policy goals, which are part of Akzo's *product life-cycle management* plan, are being applied to chlorine, a high-risk substance that is central to Akzo's business.

Forward-looking companies realize that the environment will continue to be a big issue and that they can benefit from environmental concerns. Industry can cause environmental damage, but it may also be able to repair or prevent it. Furthermore, industry makes our modern life possible. As a result, policymakers in many nations agree that efforts should focus on *sustainable business development*. In other words, national as well as international policies should balance the need to protect the environment and conserve *nonrenewable resources* with the need to produce and expand. Market-sensitive companies like Akzo see business opportunities in developing environmentally safe products and processes for the new era of sustainable development.

2. Answer the questions based on what you have learned. Use the italicized expressions in your answers.

a. In some cases, business people may confront a difficult decision: *comply with* costly environmental regulations now or risk paying for *environmental clean-up* later. How would Akzo executives make the choice? How would you make it?

b. In the European Community, the law says that polluters are *strictly liable* for the damage they cause and must clean it up. What problems might arise with enforcing this law?

c. In environmental policy, Akzo has moved from reactive *end-of-pipe solutions* to strongly proactive *product life-cycle management*. What are some of the challenges of this new policy? Why is life-cycle management of chlorine, for example, very complex?

d. *Sustainable business development* will help some businesses and some nations, but it will hurt others. Why?

C. Akzo's Corporate Rules of Conduct Concerning Safety, Health, and the Environment

Read this excerpt from Akzo's safety, health, and environmental policy publication. Discuss your reaction to the document with the class.

Activities

1. For all activities (including research, design, and development of new processes, products, plant and equipment) the effects on safety, health, and the environment shall be thoroughly investigated. Adequate measures shall be taken to reduce any adverse effects to a safe minimum.

2. Applications for investments and acquisitions shall include a paragraph on safety, health, and the environment. This paragraph shall give information about the consequences of the investment or acquisition for safety, health, and the environment, and shall also state which measures have been or will be taken to reduce any adverse effects to a safe minimum.

3. The divisions shall have an admission system for the use of new substances.

4. Akzo shall make every effort to make sure that its products—if used in accordance with Akzo's instructions or recommendations—will not have any undesirable consequences for safety, health, and the environment.

5. Akzo shall furnish all required information about the safe use, transport, storage, and disposal of its products.

6. Akzo shall inform its employees about the potential risks they are exposed to during their activities and about the measures that have been taken to minimize these risks.

The regulations for the protection of the environment shall also be part of the education and training program of the employees.

7. The employees shall be obliged to participate in safety, health, and environmental education, and to adhere to the regulations. Personal behavior in the field of safety, health, and the environment shall be part of employee performance evaluations.

8. Akzo shall work out plans to prevent accidents, where possible, together with the authorities.

PERDUE FARMS, INC.

Designing an Advertising Campaign

U n i t 9

BACKGROUND

1. Examining the Products

Read the information and look at the photographs in order to become familiar with Perdue Farms and some of its products. Then answer the questions.

Perdue Farms, Inc.

- Can be reached by mail at: Old Ocean City Road
  P.O. Box 1537
  Salisbury, Maryland 21802–1537.
- Was founded in 1920.
- Has sales of $1.23 billion.
- Is one of the largest poultry (chicken and turkey) producers in the United States.

Perdue Farms produces a wide variety of poultry products. The Perdue Done It! line features precooked products that need only reheating. From this line, we see Fun Shapes nuggets (breaded chicken pieces) and Barbecued Chicken (chicken in a spicy sauce). Perdue also produces turkey products such as the Perdue Turkey Sausages pictured here.

---

1. These chicken and turkey products are sold under the Perdue brand name. Have you seen other poultry products with brand names?
2. Notice the variety of Perdue Farms poultry products. Which chicken and turkey products are sold in your area? Which are new to you?
3. Do you prefer to buy chicken live, freshly killed, or frozen? Do you usually purchase chicken at a market, butcher shop, or supermarket? Why?

2. Gathering Data: Using a Questionnaire

The questionnaire that follows asks for the kind of information Perdue Farms executives could use to gather data about consumer preferences.

A. Use the questionnaire to find out about your classmates' attitudes toward meat and poultry. Answer the questions; then work in pairs. Ask your partner the questions and take notes on the responses.

Buying Habits and Consumer Attitudes: Meat, Poultry, and Hot Dogs

	You	Your Partner
1. Compare your consumption of meat (beef, pork, veal) to that of chicken and turkey. Which do you consume more of? Why? Consider flavor, price, availability, and healthfulness.		
2. Has your consumption of meat and poultry changed in recent years? If so, why?		
3. When you buy poultry, do you have a preference for a certain brand? If so, why?		
4. Does the color of the chicken skin influence your choice of chicken? Do you prefer whitish, blackish, or yellowish skin? Why?		
5. Do you eat hot dogs (franks)? How often?		
6. Do you buy hot dogs at the supermarket? How often?		
7. Do you consider hot dogs nutritious and healthy?		

	You	Your Partner
8. If you had a choice between beef franks and chicken franks, which would you buy for your family? Why?		
9. Does advertising (on TV or radio or in magazines or newspapers) influence your purchases of meat, poultry, or hot dogs? If so, in what ways?		

B. Discuss your reactions to the answers on the questionnaire. Did anything surprise or interest you particularly? What do the responses reveal about consumer attitudes toward meat, poultry, and hot dogs?

3. Gathering Data: Reading

Perdue Farms was one of the first U.S. poultry producers to advertise its own brand of chicken to the public. Now Perdue chicken sells well in many parts of the United States, and the company wants to develop TV ad campaigns for other products.

Read these articles to gather background data on the company and its advertising, including information to answer these questions:

- How was the Perdue Farms company built?
- How did the ad agency develop its advertising approach for Perdue Farms chicken?
- What did the successful TV ads for Perdue chicken look like?

A. Scanning for Information

Work in groups of three. Look at the Perdue Farms Fact Sheet on page 124. Each person should scan one of the three articles and take notes in the appropriate section of the outline. Then, share information so that you and your partners have the same data and can fill in the Perdue Farms Fact Sheet completely.

1. BUILDING PERDUE FARMS

Frank Perdue was born in the state of Maryland, south of Washington, D.C., in 1920, the same year his father, Arthur, founded an egg farm. Frank entered his father's business at the age of ten when he was put in charge of fifty chickens. Although it was the Great Depression and unemployment was very high, Frank earned ten to twenty dollars per month selling eggs—a decent wage for an adult. At first, he did not think he wanted to go into the family business. But in 1939, following two years of college, Frank Perdue changed his mind.

At that time, the company had three employees: Frank, his father, and one other person. They all worked long hours and the operation grew, from selling table eggs to the hatching and growing of broilers.[1] In 1948, when Frank took over leadership of the company, Perdue Farms had forty employees and was one of the largest chicken growers on the eastern shore of Maryland. As a result of special research and breeding programs, Perdue developed a high-quality bird. Swift and Armour, large meat and poultry companies, bought Perdue chickens and sold them under their own brand names.

Some years later, Perdue decided that he could market chicken under the Perdue Farms label. To get customers to recognize the name and ask for Perdue chicken, he began a tremendous effort to advertise his products on radio, TV, and in print. Instead of just buying chicken, more and more consumers became aware of the brand of chicken they bought.

Once his chicken became popular, Frank Perdue kept adding products, such as chicken and turkey parts, boneless and skinless chicken, and precooked poultry. Now Perdue is the fourth-largest poultry producer in the United States. The company employs 12,000 people, and processes over 7 million chickens each week. Every chicken is shipped fresh from the Perdue plant to poultry wholesalers and supermarket warehouses up and down the East coast and as far west as Chicago.

Retired as head of the business, Frank Perdue is involved in setting up a school of business at Salisbury State University in Maryland, where he studied, and serves on the board of directors of the National Broiler Council.

When Frank Perdue stepped down as chairman of Perdue Farms, he handed over the reins[2] to his son, James. The company has profit problems because overproduction in the industry is pushing down wholesale poultry prices in the market. To help Perdue Farms get through this downturn in the business, James Perdue is banking on[3] increased attention to quality control and strategic[4] planning. He believes that these efforts will put Perdue Farms ahead when the poultry business bounces back to higher profit levels.

1. chickens (to be cooked by broiling or roasting in the oven)
2. gave control
3. depending on
4. skillful

Perdue Farms Fact Sheet

1. Building Perdue Farms

A. Frank Perdue Builds the Business
   1. Eggs

   2. Broilers

   3. Perdue-brand chicken

   4. Retirement activities

B. James Perdue Takes Over
   1. Profit problems

   2. Future plans

2. Planning an Advertising Campaign for Perdue Chicken

A. New York as a Market
   1. Population

   2. Consumer preferences

B. Ad Campaign Research
   1. Yellow chicken skin

   2. Close supervision

   3. Frank Perdue's personal qualities

C. Ad Campaign Design
   1. Spokesperson

   2. Budget

3. Examples of TV Ads for Perdue Chicken

A. Ad Message: Perdue Chickens Are Healthy and Well-Fed
   1. Yellow color

   2. Imported feed

   3. Dessert

   4. Ventilation

B. Ad Message: Perdue Personally Supervises the Operation
   1. In a Perdue plant

   2. In a competitor's plant

C. Ad Message: Perdue Chicken Is Easy to Prepare

2. PLANNING AN ADVERTISING CAMPAIGN FOR PERDUE CHICKEN

After many years of selling his chickens to other companies, Frank Perdue decided to market his chicken under its own brand name, Perdue Farms. He chose to advertise in New York because the city is an efficient designated marketing area (DMA): There are nearly 20 million people within a sixty-mile circle around the central city. Also, New Yorkers demand high-quality products and consume a great deal of chicken. After interviewing forty advertising firms, he chose Scali, McCabe, Sloves as his agency. The executives visited Perdue Farms in Salisbury, Maryland, south of Washington, D.C., then designed an ad campaign emphasizing how Perdue chickens differ from other chickens. Featuring Frank Perdue himself, the ads have run for years with great success. . . .

One of the first things that McCabe, Scali, and Pesky did was to travel down to Salisbury to see something of Perdue's operation in order to gain an understanding of their new client and to figure out their advertising approach to his product. . . .

The first difference that the visiting admen felt they could make use of was the markedly yellow color of Perdue chickens' skin. . . .

By adding <u>marigold petals and marigold-petal extracts, leaf alfalfa, and corn-gluten meal,</u>[1] he doubled the normal level of <u>xanthophyll</u>[2] in the feed. The extra shot of xanthophyll raised the cost of the feed, and didn't itself add anything to the quality of the chickens raised on it, but it did give the birds a healthy, well-fed look.

Another impression that the men from Scali, McCabe, Sloves gained from their visit to Salisbury was that Perdue supervised the operations of his company very closely. . . .

One of the ad executives said: "Nobody had ever advertised a brand-name chicken before, and just looking at Perdue and listening to him was a new experience, too: He looked a little like a chicken himself, and he sounded a little like one, and he <u>squawked</u>[3] a lot. And about four or five weeks into the assignment <u>it just clicked</u>[4]: 'Here's the answer.'"

The answer was that Perdue himself should be the <u>spokesman</u>[5] for Perdue Farms chickens. It remained for the agency people to convince Perdue of that. They drew up a series of <u>storyboards</u>[6] for commercials featuring Perdue and presented them to him and to other top executives of his company. . . .

The commercials were instantly successful. Within a year, Perdue Farms quadrupled its TV-advertising budget, and sales of Perdue chickens in the New York metropolitan area were growing rapidly.

SOURCE: *The New Yorker*, Thomas Whiteside

1. flower petals and other plants and grains
2. yellow pigment found in green plants and egg yolk
3. cried like a bird
4. the solution became clear
5. person who speaks officially
6. outlines of the events in TV ads

3. EXAMPLES OF TV ADS FOR PERDUE CHICKEN

After many years of selling his chickens to other companies, Frank Perdue decided to market and advertise his chicken under its own brand name, Perdue Farms. A main characteristic, or keystone, of Perdue's advertising campaign was that Frank Perdue himself would speak on-camera for Perdue Farms chicken. Although he was not enthusiastic about this at first, he later came to enjoy his status as a well-known spokesperson. Here are examples of his TV ads, or spots, focusing on the healthfulness of his chickens and his personal involvement with every detail of the business....

"A chicken is what it eats," Perdue declares in one of his commercials. "And my chickens eat better than people do." By way of bolstering[1] this claim, Perdue goes on to tell viewers that he stores his own grain, mixes his own feed, and gives his chickens "nothing but pure well[2] water to drink"—and that, he says, is why "my chickens always have that healthy golden-yellow color." In another spot,... Perdue says, "They get golden-yellow corn, imported hand-picked Mexican marigold petals,[3] fresh, imported Norwegian herring.[4]" And in yet another spot, in a voiceover[5] of a shot of a full bag of meal, he adds, "My chickens even get cookies for dessert." But if chickens are subjected to "cheaper feed," poor ventilation,[6] and other treatment not up to Perdue standards, the "nice yellow color" may be absent. "So don't wonder why my chickens are so yellow," Perdue tells viewers in a number of his commercials, "wonder why some chickens are so white."

The Perdue Farms commercials have shown Perdue in a variety of situations. In one commercial he is seen walking through one of his company's plants and keeping an eye on the production lines. In another commercial he describes picking up samples of feed from other chicken raisers for quality-comparison tests.... Another commercial shows Perdue wearing swimming trunks and floating on a plastic raft in a swimming pool as several dozen good-looking young women swim and frolic nearby—this to illustrate the point that any woman in the TV audience who cooks a big Oven Stuffer Roaster at home won't have to watch over it, because "when the bird-watcher thermometer pops, it's perfect.[7]" And if you spend less time in the kitchen, Perdue tells his audience, "think of all the fun you can have."

SOURCE: *The New Yorker,* Thomas Whiteside

1. supporting
2. underground
3. flower petals
4. fish
5. narration (in which the speaker is not seen)
6. not enough fresh air
7. there is a plastic button in the chicken that opens when the meat is cooked

B. Interpreting Information

Review the information on your Perdue Farms Fact Sheet. Read the questions below. Discuss your answers and explain your opinions.

1. After years of experience in the poultry business, Frank Perdue decided to market his own Perdue-brand chicken. How did this decision affect the business?

2. Every advertising campaign seeks a main feature that cannot be stolen by competitors. In this case, the ad executives chose Frank Perdue as the keystone. Why was this a good decision?

3. The TV ad campaign identified Perdue Farms chicken as different from and better than other chicken. What qualities of Perdue chicken were emphasized?

"IF YOU PREFER MEAT TO BONE, WHY WOULD YOU BUY ANYONE ELSE'S CHICKEN?"

Frank Perdue

I've spent decades raising my Perdue breed of chickens so that they'd have smaller bones and more meat than the competition. And since Perdue chickens are also bred to be tender, juicy and delicious, more meat and less bone is exactly what you want.

Perdue birds don't become so desirable by accident. It's taken over 60 generations of breeding to get them where they are today.

So, it's no wonder, when it comes to copying my Perdue breed, the competition falls short.

What really puzzles me is why some people still buy the competitions' birds instead of mine. After all, I've never met anyone who prefers bone to meat.

PERDUE FRESH Young Chicken

Frank Perdue often appears in ads for Perdue chicken products. His favorite slogan is "It takes a tough man to make a tender chicken." What does this phrase mean? Why is it clever?

C. Reviewing Background Information and Vocabulary

Read the sentences and find the word or expression in the box that means the same as the italicized words. Then compare your answers with those of a classmate. If you disagree, consult another classmate, a dictionary, or your teacher.

a. in large quantities

b. focused on

c. support

d. depending on

e. given control

f. exposed to

g. increasing two times

h. salary (by the hour, day, week, or unit of work)

i. periods of low sales and profits

j. commercials broadcast on TV or radio

k. supervising

_____ 1. Frank Perdue got his start in the poultry business at the age of ten. His father paid him an adult *wage* to take care of fifty chickens.

_____ 2. When Frank Perdue took over the business, he began to sell poultry as well as eggs *wholesale*. With careful attention to quality, he expanded the business, first locally in the state of Maryland, then regionally in several areas of the United States.

_____ 3. Perdue introduced many innovations into the business. By *doubling* the usual amount of xanthophyll in his chicken feed, for example, he was able to produce chickens with yellowish skin.

_____ 4. Advertising executives were hired to develop an ad campaign for Perdue chicken. The Perdue Farms commercials *featured* Frank Perdue himself so that no other company could imitate them.

_____ 5. To *bolster* claims that his chickens are healthier than others, Perdue ads showed their special feed and yellow skin color.

_____ 6. The ads also said that chickens *subjected to* different conditions are not as healthy as Perdue chickens. If the skin is not yellow, the chickens probably are not fed as well.

_____ 7. Many of the TV ads showed Frank Perdue *keeping an eye on* every aspect of chicken processing. He seemed interested in each detail.

_____ 8. The Perdue chicken *spots* were so clever that Frank Perdue became famous, and so did his advertising agency.

_____ 9. Frank Perdue is now retired and has *handed over the reins* of his remarkably successful poultry business to his son, James.

_____10. Now that he is running the company, James Perdue is concerned with *downturns* in the poultry industry. To strengthen the company in good times as well as bad, he has decided to focus more attention on quality control and long-range planning.

_____11. Frank could have chosen another executive to head Perdue Farms, but he is *banking on* his son James to do the job. Frank took over from his father, so he wants James to take over from him.

PART 2

MAKING DECISIONS—DESIGNING
AN ADVERTISING CAMPAIGN

Introduction to the Problem. Frank Perdue changed the poultry market in the United States. As spokesperson on TV for his own products, he convinced consumers to choose Perdue-brand chicken and turkey. Now Perdue Farms has another product, Perdue Chicken Franks, which are made from pieces of chicken leftover from the processing of its other products. The company wants to plan an advertising campaign to promote these chicken hot dogs. The problem is that Frank Perdue does not want to appear in the ads.

Keep the problem in mind as you do the following exercises.

4. Exploring Business Culture: Cultural Values in Advertising

Read the information. Then, working in small groups, answer the questions.

Businesses spend an enormous amount of money on advertising to influence consumers. Advertising reflects cultural values because it is carefully planned to make people feel clever, important, and secure in their choices. Psychology provides some useful terms for analyzing the persuasive strategies used in ads.

Some commercials appeal to the *achievement* motive, or people's desire to do things well. This goal, or aspiration, may be expressed in ads by people doing something more competently than others or doing something unusual or difficult.

Other ads appeal to the *affiliation* motive, or the need to be with other people. In advertising, this desire may be expressed by pleasant family or social relationships, or by participation in a variety of social activities.

Another strong appeal is to people's desires to influence or control others, the *power* motive. In advertising, the message is that use of a particular product will give you power or higher social status.

Appeals to *fear* are also common in advertising. People are motivated by a strong desire to avoid fear and anxiety. The message in commercials is that failure to use a product may result in a loss or create a problem.

Finally, appeals to *sex* are very common in advertising. Commercials often use young and attractive people to sell products or imply that use of products will enhance the youthfulness and attractiveness of consumers.

Many ads combine appeals to more than one motive. The advertisers of Perdue Farms chicken found ways of appealing to several of these social aspirations and fears. It is clear, too, that most Perdue ads target women since women shopping in supermarkets are the chief consumers of Perdue products.

1. Read the descriptions of the six TV ads for Perdue chicken mentioned in the article on page 126. What strategies are used to convince consumers to buy Perdue chicken? Discuss each commercial in terms of achievement, affiliation, power, fear, and sex.

   1. "A chicken is what it eats."
   2. "They get golden-yellow corn . . . "
   3. "My chickens even get cookies."
   4. supervising production lines
   5. comparing samples of chicken feed
   6. "Think of all the fun you can have."

2. Would the Perdue ads influence you to buy Perdue Farms chicken if it were available?

3. What factors, besides advertising, might influence a consumer's choice of a product?

5. Strategies for Negotiation: Inventing Possibilities

During negotiations and meetings of all kinds, it is often helpful to consider many possibilities before actually making a choice. A common problem for business people is "either-or thinking." There is a tendency to approach a problem with the idea that either we do this, or that. In fact, it is often best to consider more choices than you may be aware of at the outset.

Here are some expressions that can help you invent possibilities:

Let's brainstorm several possibilities.
You might say this once during a meeting.

What if we were...?
Imagine yourselves in different roles, for example, as parents, children, business owners, or consumers.

What if we changed our assumptions?
Imagine a situation with different limitations, for example, more or less time, more or less money, or changes happening over time.

1.   Prepare to use the negotiating strategy. Write the phrases for inventing possibilities on cards or strips of paper. Use these expressions in the exercise.

2.   Work in small groups. Discuss one or more of these situations. When you want to invent possibilities, use an expression from your cards.

a.   A zipper maker wants to find new applications for zippers. All of the current customers are clothing manufacturers. Help invent new possibilities.

b.   An association of fruit producers in your area wants to encourage more consumption of apples and cherries. Most of the current customers are bakeries and makers of jams and jellies. Help invent new possibilities.

6. Conducting a Business Meeting: Meeting with Advertising Executives

A. Prepare for the Meeting

1. Read about the business problem.

> Perdue Farms advertisements featuring Frank Perdue have sold an enormous amount of product for the company. To help reverse a recent downturn in sales, the company wants to advertise another product: Perdue Chicken Franks. There are two immediate challenges: Frank Perdue does not want to be the spokesperson for this product, and many consumers think they do not like chicken hot dogs. At this meeting, a Perdue senior executive gets people from the company and the ad agency to share information and ideas for the new TV ad campaign.

2. Notice the format of the meeting.

Introduction

- The Perdue senior executive opens the meeting by welcoming and introducing everyone.
- The Perdue senior manager states the purposes of the meeting: to share information and ideas about a new TV ad campaign to sell Perdue Chicken Franks in New York (or in another large designated market area, DMA.)

Agenda

- Two groups of executives discuss the problem. The Perdue senior manager walks around the room and listens in on the groups.
- The Perdue senior executive elicits information and ideas from each group. When appropriate, he or she encourages the participants to invent possibilities.

Closing

- The Perdue senior manager closes the meeting by thanking everyone for participating. He or she asks the advertisers to put their ad ideas into storyboards for the next meeting.

3. Review your notes on the Perdue Farms Fact Sheet, the vocabulary, the information on business culture, and the negotiating strategy of the unit. Prepare to use this information in the meeting.

B. Conducting the Meeting

Role play the business meeting.

- Select one person to run the meeting as a Perdue senior executive. He or she will begin the meeting and follow the format described.

- Form two groups of executives, one group from Perdue Farms and the other from its ad agency. Read the role summaries. Follow the format described.

The Roles

Perdue Executives

You want a great new ad campaign. You are banking on people from your ad agency to create one. Your job is to give them high-quality product information.

- These are the important qualities of Perdue Chicken Franks.

  Compared to beef franks, Perdue Chicken Franks are higher in protein, lower in fat, and just as tasty.

  Compared to other chicken hot dogs, Perdue's are tastier and healthier.

- These are the qualities of Perdue Farms that your earlier spots have established.

  Your chickens are well-fed and have a healthy yellow color.

  You care about every detail of your operations.

- You think the market for hot dogs includes mothers, young people, and street vendors.

- (Add your own.)

Advertising Executives

You want ad ideas that draw on existing brand-name loyalty and cannot be stolen. Inventing possibilities is your specialty.

- What if you use a spokesperson in the ad campaign?

  Try Frank Perdue as before, or in the form of a younger look-alike, or in a voiceover.

  Try a younger man, for a product that appeals to young people.

  Try a mother who cares about every detail of her family's food and health.

- What if you let the product "speak" for itself?

  Try Perdue Chicken Franks saying, "We are healthy, convenient, low-cost, and from the same Perdue family of products."

  Try Perdue chickens saying, "We are well-fed. We go into Chicken Franks."

- (Add your own.)

---

7. Follow-Up Activities

A. Business Writing

1. Look at the storyboard for a possible Perdue TV spot, which was written by a student. Notice its three parts: a videoscript (left), a drawing (center), and an audioscript (right).

Asako Agency, Inc.

Client: <u>Perdue</u>
Product: <u>Perdue Chicken Franks</u>
Date: _____

Videoscript

As the scene opens, we see a beef frank sleeping on a hot dog roll.

Audioscript

The sound of snoring

A chicken frank, cheerful and active, appears next to the sleeping beef frank.

Beef frank: (Low voice, slowly and without energy) Uh, you're a new face?
Chicken frank: (Clear, energetic voice) Yes. I'm a Perdue Chicken Frank.

The camera moves in for a close-up (CU) shot of the chicken frank. It is jumping and turning around.

Beef frank voiceover (VO): Why are you so active?

2. Create a storyboard for a Perdue Chicken Franks TV spot. Complete the storyboard shown by adding three to five scenes, or design an original one. Include a videoscript, drawings, and an audioscript. Use ideas from the meeting (Exercise 6).

1. **Read the summary below. Comment on the quality of the business decisions.**

Designing an Advertising Campaign

Advertising can be an enormously powerful business tool. It is also very costly. In the case of Perdue Farms, advertising was used not only to create a company image but also to transform an industry. The investment in advertising paid for itself many times over.

Before Frank Perdue began to advertise, he and his products were unknown outside of one small area in the United States. Perdue himself decided to start by running ads about his brand-name chicken in New York, a challenging *designated marketing area* (DMA) in which to sell any brand. His clever ad people decided to feature Frank Perdue as the *spokesperson* for his own products. Not only did he look and sound somewhat like a chicken, but he was able to bolster claims for the quality of his poultry with convincing personal stories. In a series of commercials, Perdue was seen in such situations as mixing grain, giving water to the chickens, and personally supervising workers. Sometimes the camera focused on his face, in close-ups. At other times it focused on the chickens or equipment, and his voice was heard narrating in a *voiceover*. When Perdue uttered his most famous *slogan*, "It takes a tough man to make a tender chicken," he conveyed a strong message about quality and personal dedication to the consumer. The ad campaign gave the company a face and a personality, and profits skyrocketed.

So successful was the Perdue campaign that it transformed the poultry industry. The thirty-second spots inspired a great deal of *brand-name loyalty* among chicken consumers. People who used to think of fresh chicken as being all the same began to ask for chicken by name. This *brand-name awareness* forced Perdue competitors to advertise their poultry products to consumers.

Perdue Farms made advertising history. In the first sixteen years with the agency, its advertising budget for radio and television increased from $250,000 to $18 million. Perdue himself became a national celebrity. It was a surprise to the agency when Frank Perdue refused to become the spokesperson for Perdue Chicken Franks. Nevertheless, the ad people found a way to keep him as the *keystone* of the campaign without having him appear on TV. Once again, the company's investment in advertising paid off handsomely in increased sales.

2. **Answer the questions based on what you have learned. Use the italicized expressions in your answers.**

a. Why is New York an efficient *designated marketing area* (DMA) for Perdue Farms? What is the most efficient DMA in your area?

b. Test your *brand-name awareness:* Can you name two leading brands of coffee, tea, or juice? Do you have *brand-name loyalty* for any of these, or do you buy for other reasons?

c. Some chief executive officers (CEOs) have tried to imitate the Perdue advertising campaign by becoming *spokespersons* for their products, but the strategy to feature the CEO does not often work. Why not? Do you know of any senior executives who have appeared as *spokepeople* for their products? Was the strategy successful?

d. Think about a TV advertising campaign that is running now. What is the main message of the campaign? What *slogan* is used to advertise the product? What is the *keystone,* or central feature, of the campaign? Do the spots use *voiceovers,* close-ups, or other special techniques? How effective is the ad campaign?

C. Fieldwork

Report to the class on advertising strategies used in newspapers and magazines in your area.

- Find several examples of ads for food or other products.
- Discuss the ads in terms of achievement, affiliation, power, fear, sex, and any other strategies used.
- Compare the cultural values expressed in these ads to those expressed in the Perdue Farms chicken TV ads described in the unit.

CROSBY VALVE & GAGE COMPANY

Choosing a Latin American Manufacturing Base

BACKGROUND

1. Examining the Products

Read the information and look at the photographs in order to become familiar with the Crosby company and some of its products. Then answer the questions.

Crosby Valve & Gage Company

- Can be reached by mail at P.O. Box 308
  Wrentham, Massachusetts 02093.
- Was founded in 1871.
- Employs fifty sales representatives in the United States and fifty abroad.
- Has five licensing agreements in Australia, France, Italy, Spain, and England.
- Has one joint venture in Spain.

Servicemen are inspecting a Crosby safety valve. These valves are dependable, simple, and economical to manufacture. The Crosby design has become standard all over the world.

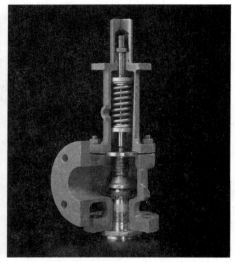

This is a cutaway of a Crosby pressure-relieving valve, which reveals the valve mechanism inside of its metal casing.

---

1. One of Crosby's major products is a line of pressure-relieving valves, or safety valves, for air, water, and steam. Safety and control valves are used together in many industries, including the petroleum processing and electric power industries. Control valves regulate the flow of liquids or gases. What is the function of safety valves?

2. Countries vary in their measurement systems, safety standards, regulatory codes (engineering standards), and import restrictions. How might these differences affect Crosby's effort to manufacture safety valves in other countries? What other factors should Crosby consider when creating an international manufacturing base for its safety valves?

2. Gathering Data: Listening

You will hear Theodore Teplow, former president and chief executive officer of the Crosby Valve & Gage Company and a graduate of the Harvard Business School. He speaks with the author about the Crosby company's international experience. Not only does Crosby make the highest quality safety valves, but it also markets them successfully all over the world.

A.   Read the questions. Then listen to the tape and write your answers. Compare your responses with those of a classmate. If you disagree, listen again.

1. Crosby was founded in 1871, and it began developing international markets in 1884. Why did Crosby go international?

2. There are a number of risks in going international. In Mr. Teplow's view, what factors caused the failure of some of Crosby's international ventures?

3. When Crosby executives consider entering a new country, they carefully study the existing industries and the overall level of economic development. Why do they look for places where Crosby can be the first local manufacturer of safety valves? What level of economic development is most favorable for the sale of safety valves?

4. According to Mr. Teplow, it is important to choose one's business partners carefully. What three characteristics does he look for in an international partner?

B.   Discuss your reaction to the interview with Theodore Teplow. Did anything surprise or interest you particularly? What do you think of his way of doing business?

3. Gathering Data: Reading

Crosby needs a market for its valves that is international in scope. It already has sales representatives in Argentina and Brazil, two industrializing economies in Latin America. Now it wants to develop a valve manufacturing base in one of these countries.

Read these research summaries, which reflect the situation in Argentina and Brazil at the time of the study. Find background data on the business environment in the two countries, including information to answer these questions:

• What is the legal, industrial, and political climate for foreign investment?
• How much competition is there in the valve market in Argentina and Brazil?
• Who are the potential business partners?

A. Scanning for Information

Work in pairs. Look at the outline called Crosby: Potential Latin American Manufacturing Bases, on page 141. Each person in the group should scan one of the two articles and take notes in the appropriate section of the outline. Then, share information so that your partner has the same data and can fill in the outline completely.

1. AN ANALYSIS OF THE POTENTIAL MARKET FOR CROSBY IN ARGENTINA

Summary. Argentina's current high level of economic activity and its generally favorable attitude toward foreign investment make it a promising market for Crosby. There is reason to believe that manufacturing Crosby's specialized safety valves could be profitable here since the private industrial sector of the Argentine economy is expanding and modernizing.

Population: 24 million

Gross National Product[1]: $17 billion

Legal Climate. Argentina welcomes private foreign investment. Licensing is encouraged. The government does not impose many legal restrictions on Argentinian companies that want to negotiate licenses to manufacture foreign products in Argentina. These licenses are legal contracts between a non-Argentine company, the licensor, and a local company, the licensee. The licensee agrees to pay an initial fee and a royalty, which is a percentage of net sales[2] of the product. The foreign company is not required to obtain government approval of such a license, nor is it required to register the license with any government agency.

The royalties on licensing agreements can range from two to six percent of net sales of the product. Companies negotiate their own royalty rates. At present, the money earned from royalties can be taken out of the country without special taxes or limits.

If foreign or Argentine companies choose to import products into Argentina, then import taxes on such products are moderate.

Political Climate. The situation is unstable. There has been a succession of military and civil regimes for a number of years in Argentina. At the time of this study, the country is run by the military. Though constitutional rule is promised, it is difficult to predict whether the country is headed for a military or civil government in the near future.

Industrial Climate. According to U.S. Department of Commerce statistics, Argentina has eighty-nine firms dealing in valves and related products. In the next five years, consumption of all types of valves is expected to rise over 40 percent, to $71 million. Valve imports are expected to remain steady, at $8 million.

Potential customers include subsidiaries[3] of U.S. and European power companies, as well as the state-controlled petroleum company of Argentina.

There is no local manufacturer of safety valves in Argentina, and Crosby-type safety valves are less than 2 percent of the total valve market.

Local Contact. Since 1937, Will L. Smith Company has been a sales representative for Crosby. Smith has sold Crosby products in Argentina, but these products have always been manufactured in the United States. Sales have varied considerably over the years, and are slow at the present time. Smith also has a limited license with Crosby to manufacture small (under three inches) bronze screwed connection valves. Under the terms of the limited license, Smith, the Argentine licensee, can manufacture only this one product out of Crosby's extensive line of products.

1. also known as GNP; the total wealth produced or earned in a country in one year
2. gross sales minus returned products
3. companies that are more than 50 percent owned by other companies

Crosby: Potential Latin American Manufacturing Bases

1. An Analysis of the Potential Market for Crosby in Argentina

A. Legal Climate
  1. Licensing

  2. Royalties

  3. Import policy

B. Political Climate
  1. Past

  2. Present and future

C. Industrial Climate, Competition
  1. Related industries

  2. Valve market

  3. Competition

D. Local Contract
  1. Current sales representative

2. An Analysis of the Potential Market for Crosby in Brazil

A. Legal Climate
  1. Licensing

  2. Royalties

  3. Import policy

B. Political Climate
  1. Past

  2. Present and future

C. Industrial Climate, Competition
  1. Related industries

  2. Valve market

  3. Competition

D. Local Contract
  1. Current sales representative

2. AN ANALYSIS OF THE POTENTIAL MARKET FOR CROSBY IN BRAZIL

Summary. In the past five years, Brazil has shown impressive economic growth and political stability. The government, however, imposes significant legal restrictions on licenses and imports.

Population: 102 million

Gross National Product[1]: $40 billion

Legal Climate. At this time, the Brazilian government is not doing a great deal to encourage foreign investment. There are several restrictions on foreign companies that want to obtain licenses to manufacture their products in Brazil. These licenses are legal contracts between a non-Brazilian company, the licensor, and a local company, the licensee. The licensee agrees to pay an initial fee and a royalty, which is a percentage of net sales[2] of all the product. At present, Brazil has significant restrictions on such licensing agreements. First, all licenses must be registered with a government agency, the National Department of Industrial Property (INPI). Currently, this agency has a five-year backlog.[3] In addition, any foreign company wishing to establish a licensing agreement with a Brazilian firm, must register the agreement with the Central Bank, which has a one-year backlog of requests.

The royalties on licensing agreements are limited to 5 percent of gross sales. Companies negotiate their own royalty rates within this limit. At present, the money earned from royalties cannot be taken out of the country for three years, unless a high tax is paid.

There are high import taxes on goods imported from abroad. If the government judges that imported goods can be replaced by locally produced Brazilian products, the import duties can be higher than 100 percent.

Political Climate. There has been a stable military government in Brazil for a number of years. The government's plan for national development is very much in favor of Brazilian business.

Industrial Climate. The U.S. Department of Commerce lists 135 firms dealing in valves and related products. There is strong growth in the industries that utilize valves, especially the petrochemical industry, which plans to spend $220 million on equipment over the next few years. Total valve imports are worth about $66 million, with safety valves comprising about $1 million of this.

Except for one low-quality licensee of a German firm, there is no Brazilian manufacturer of safety valves. There is, however, a strong presence of Japanese and European firms selling products made in their own countries. Most of them prefer dealing with suppliers from their own countries.

Local Contacts. Niagara, S.A., Brazil's largest manufacturer and importer/exporter of valves and related products, has acted as sales representative for Crosby for several years. Niagara has kept sales steady for the last few years, but has not increased them.

Crosby might also consider the Hiter partners as potential business partners. They recently came to Crosby's Massachusetts office seeking to do business. Immigrants from Spain living in Brazil, they are young, eager, and have some impressive experience: In six years the two partners have become the major manufacturer of Brazilian control valves. They have little formal education, but they do have adequate capital[4] to invest in a new business.

---

1. also known as GNP; the total wealth produced or earned in a country in one year

2. gross sales minus returned products

3. amount of material waiting to be processed

4. money and/or assets such as property or machinery

B. Interpreting Information

Review the information on your outline, Crosby: Potential Latin American Manufacturing Bases. Read each statement below. Decide whether you agree or disagree. Write *agree* or *disagree* in the blank. Work in small groups. Compare your answers with those of a classmate, and explain your opinions. There is no one right answer.

1. Overall, the legal climate of Brazil appears more favorable for foreign investment than that of Argentina.

2. A stable government, even if it is a military dictatorship, is better for business than an unstable government; therefore, the political climate in Brazil is better.

3. Though the Argentine market may be slightly smaller, it looks better for Crosby because there is less competition in the safety valve market.

4. The local contact in Argentina looks more promising as a business partner for this new project because the relationship is older.

Here you see a typical safety relief valve installation in a U.S. petrochemical plant. Crosby designs valves for all media and the full range of pressure/temperature possibilities. Technically, safety valves are used on steam, relief valves on liquid, and safety relief and pressure relief valves on gas. One of Crosby's advertising slogans is "Nobody handles pressure better." Can you explain the play on words?

C. Reviewing Background Information and Vocabulary

Read the sentences and find the word or expression in the box that means the same as the italicized words. Then compare your answers with those of a classmate. If you disagree, consult another classmate, a dictionary, or your teacher.

a. unable to survive

b. size

c. improved models

d. becoming

e. in face-to-face conversation

f. ended

g. make worthwhile

h. establish

i. an amount of material waiting to be processed

j. show signs of possible future success

k. change . . . into

_____ 1. Crosby's main product is safety valves, which, with control valves, are used widely in petroleum processing and power industries. The company needs a market which is international in *scope* because the domestic market for these valves is too small and unpredictable.

_____ 2. International marketing is a critical business strategy for Crosby. The company cannot afford to keep developing new and better valves if the products do not sell. Only strong sales *warrant* continued investment in research and development.

_____ 3. *Going* international requires a series of complex decisions and changes in a company.

_____ 4. According to former Crosby Chief Executive Officer Theodore Teplow, it is a good business idea to spend a lot of time *one-on-one* with your potential partner before signing an agreement.

_____ 5. Crosby is always improving its products. If customers have older valves, they may need to buy *upgrades*.

_____ 6. Crosby's licensing agreement in Australia did not work because the original licensee sold the company. Crosby executives decided to *convert* the manufacturing license back *into* a sales representative agreement, which would not be as risky.

_____ 7. Later, Crosby *terminated* the Australian sales representation. The company had merged with another and the new owners were not interested enough in the line.

_____ 8. One Crosby joint venture was not managed well. When it became economically *unviable*, requiring a great deal of added investment, Crosby decided to close it down.

_____ 9. Some countries try to protect local industry by requiring international businesses to register their agreements. This procedure can take years if there is *a backlog* at a government registration agency.

_____10. In the case of foreign investment, governments may *impose* a number of retrictions. For example, a government may require that foreign investors register their licenses with a central bank.

_____11. Despite government restrictions, a foreign market may *look promising* if the political situation or potential partners are strong. There are many factors to consider when investing abroad.

MAKING DECISIONS—CHOOSING A LATIN AMERICAN MANUFACTURING BASE

Introduction to the Problem. After studying the research summaries on Argentina and Brazil, Crosby executives have decided that they will take the risk of establishing a manufacturing base for safety valves, but in only one of the two countries. The problem is to decide which one. They also must decide whether to pursue a licensing or a joint venture agreement in that country, and with whom.

Keep the problem in mind as you do the following exercises.

4. Exploring Business Culture: International Licensing and Joint Venture Agreements

Read the information. Work in small groups to answer the questions.

Crosby already has sales representatives in Argentina and Brazil who sell Crosby valves, but executives at the company want to expand sales by developing a manufacturing base in Latin America. The executives must decide whether to pursue this goal through a licensing or a joint venture agreement. There are risks and benefits involved in each of these arrangements.

In a licensing agreement, the licensor has no ownership of the licensee in the other country, and therefore has little control of the operation. The licensee pays an initial one-time fee, plus royalties, which are an agreed-on percentage of the product sales. At Crosby, a license is usually granted for a fifteen-year period. A license is not as risky as a joint venture. It is often used when a company has similar products, so that existing machinery may be used to manufacture the licensed product.

In contrast, a joint venture agreement requires a great deal of involvement with the business partner. Both buyer and seller contribute to the business, and they share ownership. One company, for example, might supply the technology and money for the enterprise, while the other company might supply the manpower and machinery. In U.S. joint ventures, the ownership is frequently split 51 percent to 49 percent, with the U.S. company retaining control. A joint venture is riskier, but it is potentially more profitable than a license since the company not only earns royalties but also dividends, which are returns on its whole investment.

Whatever agreement is selected, Theodore Teplow advises that business partners be chosen carefully. One should talk with the potential partners one-on-one and try to determine whether they share one's interests, values, and enthusiasm for the business.

1. What are the risks and benefits of licensing agreements as compared to joint ventures?
2. In your area, do you know whether licenses or joint ventures with international partners are more common? Do you know what kinds of businesses have these international agreements?
3. In doing business internationally, how important is one's choice of a business partner?

5. Strategies for Negotiation: Giving Feedback

This exercise helps you practice giving feedback, a strategy that allows managers to maintain a positive attitude even when they do not completely agree with the result of someone else's actions. You can separate the good ideas from the not-so-good ones and, at the same time, avoid conflict and hurt feelings. The exercise also introduces some sensitive cross-cultural issues that may arise in international business.

Here are some expressions you can use to give feedback:

Specify merits

What I like about your plan is...

Your plan is good in that it...

Specify concerns

What concerns me about your plan is...

A potential problem with your plan is that...

NOTES

- Make your feedback as specific as possible.

- Try giving the positive feedback first, then people are often more willing to listen to the concerns.

1.   **Prepare to use the negotiating strategy. Write the expressions for giving feedback on cards or strips of paper. Use the expressions in the exercise below.**

2.   **Work in small groups. Discuss one or more of these situations. When you want to give feedback, use an expression from your cards.**

a.   In the United States, it is illegal to pay fees to purchasers to obtain contracts. It is considered bribery. In some countries where Crosby wants to do business, such fees are a common business practice. What should Crosby executives do? Suggest a plan of action, and give feedback on it.

b.   Crosby valves have many applications for the military. Imagine that Crosby executives have heard a rumor that their products are being used to develop weapons in another country. How can Crosby executives determine whether this is true? Suggest a plan of action, and give feedback on it.

6. Conducting a Business Meeting: An In-House Strategy Session

A. Preparing for the Meeting

1. Read about the business problem.

Crosby Executives have carefully studied the climate for investment in both Argentina and Brazil. Now they must decide where to develop a manufacturing base. The executives are eager to act since they know the advantage of being the first safety valve manufacturer in a country.

- Should Crosby pursue an agreement in Argentina or Brazil?
- Who should their business partners be?
- Should Crosby pursue a joint venture or a licensing agreement?

2. Notice the format of the meeting.

Introduction
- Mr. Teplow, chief executive officer, opens the strategy session by greeting everyone.
- He states the purpose of the meeting: to decide which country, type of agreement, and partner to pursue in Latin America.

Agenda
- Each group of executives discusses the risks and benefits, potential partners, and most favorable investment agreement. Mr. Teplow moves around the room and listens in on the groups.
- Mr. Teplow asks each group to present its position. Then, he asks the executives to discuss the possibilities freely to determine what is best for the company. Participants are free to change their positions. When appropriate, Mr. Teplow and other participants give feedback.

Closing
- Mr. Teplow summarizes the reasons behind the group's choice of county, partner, and business agreement.
- He closes the session by thanking the participants and mentioning that he will soon write a business proposal with a recommended plan of action.

3. Review your notes on the Crosby outline, the vocabulary, the information on business culture, and the negotiating strategy in the unit. Prepare to use this information in the strategy session.

B. Conducting the Meeting

Role play the strategy session.

- Select one person to run the meeting as Theodore Teplow, chief executive officer. Mr. Teplow will conduct the meeting, following the format described above.

- Form two groups of Crosby executives, one in favor of Brazil and the other in favor of Argentina. Read the role summaries below. Follow the meeting format described.

The Roles

Crosby Executives in Favor of Argentina

You believe that Argentina looks more promising as a place to develop a manufacturing base for Crosby, despite some disadvantages.

- The legal climate is not overly restrictive. Either licensing or joint venture agreements could be arranged.

- The industrial climate offers strong growth potential, and there are a number of related industries. There is no local manufacturer of safety valves to compete with you.

- The political climate is somewhat uncertain.

- Your sales representative, Will Smith, is a potential partner, but the elder Mr. Smith is ready to have his sons take over. Their motivation and business sense is unclear.

- *(Add your own.)*

Crosby Executives in Favor of Brazil

You believe that, despite some disadvantages, Brazil is the more promising country for Crosby's Latin American investment plan.

- The legal climate appears complex and restrictive. It looks like a licensing agreement cannot pay enough royalty to be worth it. A joint venture is possible, but riskier.

- The industrial climate offers strong growth potential, and there are plenty of related industries. There is one low-quality licensee of a German firm, but otherwise no local manufacturer of safety valves.

- The political climate has been stable for several years, but the country is run by the military.

- Your partner for many years has been Niagara, S.A., but the company may soon be taken over by two sons with questionable interest in it. The Hiter partners are a possibility since they have six years' experience making control valves.

- *(Add your own.)*

7. Follow-Up Activities

A. Business Writing

Write a business proposal recommending which country, agreement, and partner Crosby should pursue in Latin America. Support your recommendation with data from the unit. Organize your proposal using the format below. Be sure to use the headings in your proposal.

The Market for Crosby in (*your recommendation*)

Summary

(Under this heading, write one paragraph summarizing your reasons for recommending this country. Then state the type of business agreement you recommend, with your reasons. Finally, state your choice of business partner.)

Legal Climate

(Compare the business climate in Argentina and Brazil from a legal point of view. Discuss why your choice is better than the other.)

Political Climate

(Compare the business climate in Argentina and Brazil from a political point of view. Discuss why your choice appears better.)

Industrial Climate

(Compare the business climate for Crosby in Brazil and Argentina from an industrial point of view. Discuss why your choice appears better.)

Local Contacts

(Compare the possible business partners in Brazil and Argentina. State why your choice seems the best for Crosby.)

B. Putting the Problem in Perspective: Applying Business Concepts

1. Read the summary of the business problem. Comment on the quality of Crosby's business decisions.

Choosing an International Manufacturing Base

Establishing a *manufacturing base* overseas, in contrast to a sales representation, requires a thorough research and decision-making process. Crosby executives spent several years gathering information about the investment climate in Argentina and Brazil before deciding where to invest.

Crosby's top managers were looking for an *industrializing economy* with strong growth and a large enough GNP and industrial base to warrant local production of safety valves. They also were looking to be the first local manufacturer of safety valves in order to develop a strong *after market*, which is a demand for service, parts, and upgrades on valves that are already installed. Both Argentina and Brazil satisfied these conditions, so Crosby executives moved on to examine how local laws and politics might affect investment. Argentina seemed to offer fewer legal restrictions, yet the government at the time was somewhat unpredictable. They had to consider which set of circumstances looked more promising for business.

At the same time, Crosby executives had to consider their potential partners. They were faced with a choice between expanding their relationship with unexciting but known partners, Smith in Argentina or Niagara in Brazil, or taking a chance on the Hiter partners in Brazil, who were highly motivated but also were high-risk partners by ordinary standards. There was a third option, too: searching for completely new partners.

The decision about which country and which partner came together, leaving the executives with one last choice: what kind of agreement should they make? A *license* would give Crosby less control and less profit potential, but it would also have less risk. In contrast, a *joint venture* would give Crosby more control and potentially more profit, but would be riskier. A joint venture would require a closer relationship with the Latin American partners.

The decision as to where, with whom, and how to invest in Latin America has made a big difference for Crosby. Unlike most American companies at the time, Crosby decided to invest in Brazil. They negotiated a highly successful joint venture with the Hiter brothers, who have turned out to be exceptionally good business partners. Since the original agreement proved so viable, the scope of the company's involvement has grown. Currently, over 55 percent of its revenues come from out-of-country sales, and a good portion of this figure comes from sales in Latin America.

2. Answer the questions based on what you have learned. Use the italicized expressions in your answers.

a. Crosby already had sales representation in Latin America for many years. Why did company executives want to convert this into a *manufacturing base* for safety valves?

b. Why do *industrializing economies* offer better business opportunities for Crosby than industrialized economies? What other industrializing countries might be good markets for Crosby valves? On the other hand, what restrictions might these economies impose?

c. Why is the *after market* so important for Crosby products? What other kinds of products have an *after market*?

d. A *license* to manufacture Crosby valves requires the transfer of technology. What risks might be associated with the granting of *licenses*? How can companies minimize or reduce these risks?

e. *Joint ventures* require close cooperation between the two partners. Why might some executives want to share the profits and risks more equally with an international partner? What is your personal philosophy in this matter?

Appendix A

ANSWER KEY FOR REVIEWING BACKGROUND INFORMATION AND VOCABULARY

Unit 1

1. j   2. h   3. f   4. a   5. i   6. d   7. e   8. c   9. g   10. b

Unit 2

1. d   2. g   3. i   4. h   5. j   6. c   7. e   8. a   9. f   10. b

Unit 3

1. e   2. g   3. a   4. f   5. b   6. i   7. c   8. j   9. k   10. d   11. h

Unit 4

1. e   2. d   3. g   4. h   5. f   6. b   7. i   8. c   9. j   10. k   11. a

Unit 5

1. e   2. g   3. c   4. j   5. f   6. d   7. i   8. h   9. b   10. a

Unit 6

1. f   2. e   3. g   4. d   5. h   6. c   7. i   8. b   9. j   10. a

Unit 7

1. i   2. b   3. e   4. c   5. f   6. j   7. h   8. g   9. a   10. d

Unit 8

1. c   2. i   3. b   4. g   5. h   6. j   7. f   8. d   9. e   10. a   11. k

Unit 9

1. h   2. a   3. g   4. b   5. c   6. f   7. k   8. j   9. e   10. i   11. d

Unit 10

1. b   2. g   3. d   4. e   5. c   6. k   7. f   8. a   9. i   10. h   11. j

INFORMATION FOR EXERCISE 5 PAIRED ACTIVITIES

Unit 1: Kentucky Fried Chicken Corporation

5. Strategies for Negotiation: Interrupting to Ask a Question or Make a Comment

Work in pairs. Student A has information. Student B does not. Student A reads aloud the information below. Student B listens and adds details to the outline on page 11. When either student needs to interrupt to ask a question or make a comment, he or she should use an expression from the cards.

Student A reads this information.

Key Events in KFC History

The internationally known company of Kentucky Fried Chicken began very quietly. Harland Sanders, who was later to become Colonel [/kernel/] Sanders, came from Kentucky, a state in the southern part of the United States. He was a poorly educated man with an undistinguished work history. His entire life changed when, in 1930, at the age of forty, Sanders opened a restaurant in Corbin, Kentucky. The featured dish at this original KFC outlet was fried chicken prepared according to Sander's original recipe.

Sales took off. The chicken became so famous that the governor of Kentucky made Sanders a colonel, which is an honorary title in Kentucky. In the mid-1950s, when business at the restaurant was reduced by a new highway through Corbin, Colonel Sanders decided to begin franchising his secret recipe. Within ten years, there were more than 600 KFC restaurants.

In 1964, at the age of 74, Colonel Sanders decided to sell the company to another Kentucky businessman for $2 million. Seven years later, the new owners sold it to the Heublein Company for $275 million. Despite the sale and resale of the company, the recipe for the chicken is still a trade secret. It is kept under eleven locks in a fireproof, bombproof vault at KFC headquarters in Louisville, Kentucky. Only Harland Sanders and a few others know what really makes the chicken "finger lickin' good."

Unit 6: Airbus Industrie and the Boeing Company

5. Strategies for Negotiation: Identifying Areas of Agreement

Work in pairs. Student A presents the position below to Student B. Student B listens, then presents another position. Negotiate an agreement between the two neighbors. When you want to identify areas of agreement, use an expression from your cards.

Student A presents this position.

A Dispute between Neighbors

You are a busy executive with a high-pressure job. The sound of the piano coming from the apartment above every night is driving you crazy.

- You leave early and get home late, so you need rest in the evening.
- Although you enjoy classical music, you do not want to be forced to listen to the same pieces over and over.
- A thick rug under the instrument and a closed piano lid would muffle the sound.
- Since you work long hours, your neighbor should be able to practice when you are away.

Unit 7: Kidselebration

5. Strategies for Negotiation: Eliciting More Information

Work in pairs. Student A has information about Idea 1; Student B should not look at that information. Student A gives the information about Idea 1 to Student B, one piece at a time. Student B elicits each piece of information, using expressions from the cards. Finally, discuss your opinion of the business idea.

Then, Student B gives information about Idea 2 to Student A, one piece at a time. Student A elicits each piece of information, using expressions from the cards. Again, discuss your opinion of the business idea.

Student B uses this information.

Idea 2: You work for Kidselebration. You want to develop a personalized storybook to tie in with the Kidselebration story tape, *Name Tales*. Try to get your business associate interested in this idea by revealing one detail at a time.

- My idea is to develop a *Name Tales* personalized storybook.

- First, we could get an artist to design a book of pictures to illustrate the *Name Tales* story. For a boy, it would be pictures of a prince. For a girl, it would be a princess. All of the faces would be blank.

- The idea is that the face would be filled in with that of the individual child.

- The face could be completed with either a photo of the child or the child's drawing of his or her own face. What do you think of this idea? Can it work?

Unit 8: Akzo n.v.

5. Strategies for Negotiation: Interrupting for Clarification

Work in pairs. Student A will work with Issue 1 on page 112. Student A reads the information about Issue 1 to Student B. Student B listens carefully. Student B should not look at Issue 1. The information contains some nonsense words. When Student B needs clarification, he or she interrupts Student A, using expressions from the cards. When Student A repeats the sentence, he or she substitutes meaningful words for the nonsense words. These meaningful words are found in the footnotes.

Then, switch roles. Student B works with Issue 2 following the same procedure. Finally, discuss both issues.

Student B reads this information.

Issue 2: Exporting Hazardous Waste

Hazardous waste is an important environmental issue. It is especially important to badada.[1] Much of the country rests on water and is densely populated. If waste is not carefully managed, it can get into doodle[2] and soil. As a result, the Dutch government watches all industries. It makes sure that wastes are carefully disposed of.

The Dutch believe that the European Community must strictly control the movement of malala[3] among member nations. The Dutch want the European Community to have a policy of "prior informed consent." This means that the receiving country would have to do two things before the waste arrived. It would have to agree to receive the hazardous waste. Also, it would have to show that it can moola[4] the waste in a responsible way. The purpose of this policy is to prevent people from making money by transporting hazardous waste into other countries.

1. the Netherlands
2. water supplies
3. hazardous waste
4. dispose of

Appendix C
NEGOTIATING STRATEGIES

Unit 1: Kentucky Fried Chicken

Interrupting to Ask a Question or Make a Comment

Interrupting to Ask a Question
- Excuse me for interrupting, but...
- Sorry, may I ask a question?

Interrupting to Make a Comment
- If I can just add a point...
- Excuse me. I'd like to comment on that.

Unit 2: Johnson & Johnson

Answering Difficult Questions

Paraphrase Questions
- In other words, you're asking...
- So, what you want to know is...

Repeat Your Message
- And that brings us to the main issue here.
- So, you can see that the point is...

Unit 3: Ben & Jerry's Homemade

Conceding a Point

- Granted that...However,...
- Admittedly,...
- You're right about that. Still,...

Unit 4: Levi Strauss & Co.

Expressing Disagreement and Doubt

- I'm concerned that...
- Maybe we need to look at...
- I'm not completely convinced...

Unit 5: Stew Leonard's Dairy Store

Building on Someone Else's Idea

- And, to add to your idea...
- And, what if...
- Yes, and...

Unit 6: Airbus Industrie and the Boeing Company

Identifying Areas of Agreement

- What seem to be our areas of agreement?
- What are your priorities? These are ours...
- We both seem to be upset about this matter. Clearly, it's important to both of us.

Unit 7: Kidselebration, Inc.

Eliciting More Information

- I'd like to know more about that.
- Could you explain what you mean by...?
- Really? That's interesting. What exactly do you have in mind?

Unit 8: Akzo, N.V.

Interrupting for Clarification

- I'm sorry, I didn't [couldn't] catch what you said. Could you say it again, please?
- Excuse me, I didn't [couldn't] hear what you said. Would you mind repeating it?

Unit 9: Perdue Farms, Inc.

Inventing Possibilities

- Let's brainstorm several possibilities.
- What if we were...?
- What if we changed our assumptions?

Unit 10: Crosby Valve & Gage Company

Giving Feedback

Specify Merits
- What I like about your plan is...
- Your plan is good in that it...

Specify Concerns
- What concerns me about your plan is...
- A potential problem with your plan is that...

TAPESCRIPT

Unit 2: Johnson & Johnson Consumer Products, Incorporated
Making Ethical Decisions in Business

You will hear the president of Johnson & Johnson, David Clare, talk with a radio journalist about a tragic event: Seven people in the Chicago area died when they took Extra-Strength Tylenol, a common pain-relieving medicine made by Johnson & Johnson. Someone had opened the capsules and poisoned them with cyanide. Mr. Clare discusses the shocking incident and how people at his company responded to it.

Read the questions. Then listen to the tape and write your answers. Compare your responses with those of a classmate. If you disagree, listen again.

David Freudberg:	J&J is a household name, famous for its health products from Band Aids to baby oil. They make a big thing at Johnson & Johnson of their credo statement, a four-paragraph guiding philosophy that outlines a commitment to business integrity.
	All of which was well and good when, in the fall of 1982, a reporter from Chicago telephoned the company headquarters. He wanted reaction to the stunning news that J&J's leading product, Tylenol capsules, had apparently been contaminated with lethal poison. The president of Johnson & Johnson is David Clare:
David Clare:	The climate was one of sheer unbelieving that this had happened. The shock, absolute unhappiness associated with the obvious fact that people were dying, that they were dying potentially through the use of one of our products, and we just didn't know what had happened. We did not know how extensive it was, what the cause was, what the problem was in any dimension. It appeared to be localized, but we weren't sure.
DF:	On the market at that time, Johnson & Johnson had no less than $100 million dollars' worth of Tylenol. The process of recalling so vast an output would cost J&J stockholders a fortune, but, referring to the credo statement, the company is required to place a higher priority on the needs of consumers. And there were other questions in determining a response to the crisis.
DC:	We were in an ethical dilemma from the standpoint that—at least there were those who were arguing you should not withdraw because all you're going to do is demonstrate to some sick individual that they can have a major, nationwide impact on a major product through their individual action at some locality. So there was the argument we should not withdraw. And that was discussed for a period of about forty-eight to seventy-two hours as we argued: what was the right thing to do? And finally came down on the side there was no choice from our standpoint: We had to act to protect the public, whether it was more widespread than it appeared to be or whether it was a condition which could be repeated by other copycats using our product. So that first and foremost, we had to protect the public.
DF:	Was there not a feeling that the public, given all of the notariety about this tragic series of poisonings, would have on its own stopped buying Tylenol anyway?
DC:	They did. But, what we had to do was, through the dramatic nature of a nationwide recall, was clearly demonstrate that we wanted the product out of their homes; we wanted the product out of the shelves, just on the off chance that they might have some contaminated product. In the 8 million or so bottles that we looked at, we did find two that were contaminated. You could argue that that may have saved some lives.
	We were reacting to a set of circumstances, and we were reacting against those circumstances with a set of principles. The first principle of which is: You have to act in every way to protect the consumer,

and to do it, in our judgment, to do it promptly in the Tylenol example, was the only way we could do it. Now, we think, ultimately, it turned out to also be good for business, not only for J&J and the business of Tylenol, or J&J, and the image of it as responsible business citizens, but also we had inherited a very strong reputation with the consumer.

Reprinted by permission of the publisher, from *Corporate Conscience,* ©1986 David Freudberg. Published by the American Management Association, NY. All rights reserved.

Unit 3: Ben & Jerry's Homemade, Incorporated
Developing a Compensation Policy

You will hear a tape about Ben Cohen and Jerry Greenfield, two old friends who decided to go into the ice cream business together. "Caring capitalism," which describes Ben and Jerry's unusual and highly successful approach to business, is discussed.

Read the questions. Then listen to the tape and write your answers. Compare your responses with those of a classmate. If you disagree, listen again.

Narrator:	Ben and Jerry didn't always have their heads on top of a pint of ice cream. The story really begins with a five-dollar correspondence course on ice cream manufacturing that Ben and Jerry took back in 1977. They spent the next year experimenting and perfecting their recipes.
Jerry:	We wanted to make ice cream just like you'd make it at home. It had to be richer, creamier than regular ice cream.
Ben:	And heavy, really heavy. We learned about all the air that most manufacturers pump into their ice cream, and we said we're not going to do it. Ben & Jerry's would be dense, solid, and heavy. Kind of like us.
Narrator:	Finally, the recipes were ready. Ben and Jerry gathered some of their friends and all the money they could get their hands on and converted an abandoned gas station in Burlington, Vermont, into the original Ben & Jerry's Ice Cream Shop. It opened on May 5, 1978. Their chunk-intensive ice cream was developing quite a reputation, and so were Ben and Jerry themselves. Ben and Jerry decided early on that their business would be as different as their ice cream.
Jerry:	If it's not fun, why do it?
Ben:	Business has a responsibility to give back to the community.
Narrator:	By 1981, Ben and Jerry realized that winters in Vermont were quite beautiful, but not particularly good for ice cream sales. Then, Ben got an idea.
Ben:	Hey, Jer. What if you start packing the ice cream in pints, and then I could sell them to the mom and pop stores that I'm passing on the way to the restaurants. I'll bet people would buy a pint of Heath Bar Crunch.
Narrator:	Sales took off immediately. Within three months, 150 stores in the state carried Vermont's finest all-natural ice cream, and Ben & Jerry scoop shops began sprouting up. In 1985, as Ben & Jerry's hit the New York market, a new flavor was born: New York Superfudge Chunk was a super-fudgy chocolatey ice cream with pecans, walnuts, chocolate-covered almonds, and dark and white chocolate chunks, mmm. Soon, the demand for Ben & Jerry's Ice Cream began to outstrip supply. To handle the increase in production, the boys decided to build a real ice cream plant. The problem was how to finance it. Ben and Jerry discovered an obscure Vermont law that enabled them to register as

stockbrokers and sell shares in the company. It became Vermont's first-ever in-state public stock offering.

Ben: We wanted to make the community the owners of the business. That way, as the business prospered, the community would automatically prosper.

Jerry: We had a minimum purchase of only $126, so that almost anyone could take part. And, at the end of the offering, 1 out of every 100 Vermont families owned stock in Ben & Jerry's.

Narrator: The company has adopted a unique three-part mission statement: dedicated to social, economic, and product quality. Chocolate Fudge Brownie Ice Cream uses brownies baked at the Grayston Bakery in Yonkers, New York. The bakery provides jobs to underskilled or homeless people. The second part of the mission's statement confirms Ben & Jerry's commitment to quality products.

Man: As you walk into the production floor, it's easy to sense that the production workers take a lot of pride in the ice cream that they make. They feel that they make the best ice cream in the world.

Narrator: The third part of the mission statement concerns the company's finances.

Woman: We have something different here, called the "compressed salary ratio." And, in essence, it recognizes everyone's value and worth to the company.

Jerry: The issue is how much more is the Chief Executive making than the line-level workers. And I don't see any way that you can justify somebody making a million or more dollars a year when their line-level workers aren't making enough money to afford a house.

Narrator: Ben & Jerry's believes in the concept of "caring capitalism." The company's three-part mission statement encourages employees to integrate a concern for the community in every day-to-day business decision that they make. Caring capitalism makes serving the community just as important as making a profit and making great ice cream.

©Ben & Jerry's Homemade, Inc. Reprinted by permission.

Unit 5: Stew Leonard's Dairy Store Satisfying the Supermarket Customer

You will hear Stew Leonard and one of his associates describe the Stew Leonard approach to supermarket sales. This unusual approach combines efficiency, customer service, and fun. The approach works: An average of 100,000 shoppers buy $2 million dollars worth of groceries at the store each week.

Read the questions. Then listen to the tape and write your answers. Compare your responses with those of a classmate. If you disagree, listen again.

Stew Leonard: We started out in the store saying that we were not going to compromise on the quality. In other words, we were going to build a business based on quality. And we figured that if we could sell fresh milk—so fresh that it's right out of the cow, practically—no one could sell it fresher. You'd come right to the dairy to buy the milk. So you start with the quality, and then once you sell the quality, if you can keep the profit down and try to get the volume to come, it starts to work with itself. It starts to be a tremendous benefit because now you've got fresh quality and the customers are coming back and they're giving you volume and the volume enables you to keep your price down. And if you don't get greedy, if you want to just keep your expenses down and just keep generating high volume, then it works out.

One of the things that we're doing here: We're bottling the milk in the back, and the milk in the dairy plant, then the milk is coming out on the conveyor right out of the refrigerator. Now, all this milk will be sold today. There's this tremendous efficiency in this building. Not only are you making the products right here, but you're selling them right here with a minimum of handling. The customers take the cartons out of the cases. In a normal supermarket, you'd have to take them out of the cases. The stock boy would have to load the shelves and bring them from the back room. Here, everything is going right from the plant right to the customer. You'll see that over and over again with tremendous efficiency.

Stew Leonard's Executive:

We have a saying: You know, if you wouldn't take it home to your mother, let's not put it out on our shelves for our customers. And so we only buy top quality. And we can buy it and sell it cheaper than our competition because we cut out the middleman. We bring it direct here. There's only one unload. Most of the other companies will buy the same trailer, but they send it to a distribution center. They unload it, they reload it into trucks for the various stores. We bring it right here. This is our distribution center.

SL:

What we do is we go right to California and we get trailerloads of fresh produce right out in the produce country. We bring it in and rather than have it in normal display cases, we sell so much we need the product right behind it and constantly turning it over. 20 percent of the items in a supermarket bring 80 percent of the sales, just imagine. So what we have done here is we have taken and just taken those 20 percent and said, hey, let's just sell them. What are they? They're the basics: the milk, the bread, the eggs. There are not twenty-seven kinds of melons. I'm not saying there isn't a place for a store that sells twenty-seven melons. We don't. We want to find out that four of those melons do 80 percent of the business so we would go buy the four melons—which we have done and made a big display. People say to me constantly, "Are you crazy only selling 700 items? If you sold 15,000 items, we would buy all of the items here at the store." That's probably true, but then we would be like a supermarket, we'd have to reduce all of our displays. You couldn't have giant displays anymore, like this. You'd have to have little cans and little junk all over the place there, you know.

The concept behind this is by concentrating and focusing on a few items, we're able to buy them better or make them ourselves and then pass on savings and quality and freshness to the customer.

Now what's the disadvantage of that? Big disadvantage: Every single one of our customers, including my own wife, must go to my competitor's store every single week. Now what does that do to us? That keeps us on the ball.

Unit 7: Kidselebration, Incorporated
Expanding a Small Children's Products Business

You will hear an interview with Debbie and Peter Roth, owners and creators of Kidselebration, Incorporated, a small children's products business. They discuss with the author what makes their products distinctive, how the business has changed their lives, and what advice they would give to others who are thinking of starting a small business. You will also hear a sample of one of their major products, *Names Tunes*, a personalized song tape for children.

Read the questions. Then listen to the tape and write your answers. Compare your responses with those of a classmate. If you disagree, listen again.

Frances Boyd:

Good morning, Peter and Debbie. Thank you for coming to talk today. I wanted to ask you, as founders of Kidselebration, what you think is special about your company. What's distinctive about it?

Debbie Roth:

I think it's the fact that the goal of the company is to make children feel good about themselves, to build their self-esteem and their confidence. Watching how children are affected by the tape is probably the biggest testimony to that goal. Six year-olds, five-year-olds, six-year-olds are probably the oldest kids that enjoy the tape and they—it's a very egocentric age—and they hear their names, they just light up. At the other end of the age scale, you've got infants—four- and six-month olds—who are just learning words and probably the first word that they learn is their name. We've heard from parents that it's a tape they enjoy listening to also.

FB:

Why did you decide to start Kidselebration?

Peter Roth:

For the most part, when you want to start your own company, it's to get more control over your life. I already had control over my life in the sense that I had worked for myself all my life before that, and I wasn't looking for that so much as I was looking to build a future for my family. I wanted to build a company that would become bigger than me, would have a lot of people working for it, would have a product or a service that could be sold and managed when I'm not around, and therefore I could still make money even if I was on vacation or I was sick, or something like that. And, at the end, I could sell the company if I wanted and it would be worth something to somebody else because it wouldn't be selling me, it would be selling something that I created. And so I think when people build, start their own companies, that the factor of it being an asset I think is very important and what they can do with it to create value.

FB:

Return on your investment, so to speak. How has building Kidselebration affected your life-style?

DR:

Well, as Peter said, he went from one entrepreneurial type of work to this. In my case, when he first started Kidselebration six years ago, at that point I was working full-time for a pension company, managing retirement benefits for colleges and universities around the country. For me, I think the adjustment has been . . . the biggest adjustment in that change for me was the life-style adjustment, was the fact that I wasn't going off to work every day, with my commuting time to consider and a lunch hour all to myself. I would give anything to have a lunch hour now! And a babysitter! And all the things that I don't have now. But the big thing that I have now, which I realized recently when I considered going back into corporate life, is a tremendous amount of flexibility. And when you have small children that's . . . for me, that was essential. For us, as a team, as partners—both husband and wife and also in the business—the biggest challenge is to juggle our work life and our home life because they are so intimately intertwined.

FB:

Yeah, now you've had six years of experience building this business, would you have any advice for someone who might want to start a business?

PR:

Well, the first advice would be to understand the risk that you're taking and feel, try to feel within yourself that it's the right thing. There are opportunities that come across and you can say, "Oh, I could take it. I might not take it. Hey, why not?" I'm not sure that those are the things that work out as well as what you feel passionate about. Another thing I would say has to do with the people that you work with and talk to. And a lot of people are very polite and a lot of people will answer you in a way that they think you want to be answered. And those are not the people you want to speak to. You want to speak to people who will be judgmental and critical.

FB:

Do you think now you have a different feeling about the risk than you did six years ago? Is it less of a risk now than it was then?

PR:

There are different kinds of risk. I don't feel a risk with win or lose. I now feel risky in the gray areas in between.

DR:

It's not a question of whether the business is going to survive or not, or come crashing down tomorrow.

PR:

We will survive. We're not worried about our survival as much as we're concerned about the quality of what we're doing, and the risk that we're taking with that quality.

Hello, Benjamin, how do you do?
I'm going to sing some songs for you.
Some fast songs and slow songs and funny songs too,
So join in and sing along and have some fun too.

We're going to sing about Benjamin
We're going to sing about Benjamin
We're going to sing about Benjamin
A special boy.

From when he gets up in the morning
Until he sleeps in the evening,
It's a special world for Benjamin
'Cause he's a special boy.

Unit 8, Akzo n.v.
Responding to Environmental Concerns in Europe

You will hear an interview with John Behan, a specialist in environmental law and a lawyer for Akzo America, Incorporated. He discusses with the author Akzo's environmental policies and some major concepts in environmental regulation.

Read the questions. Then listen to the tape and write your answers. Compare your responses with those of a classmate. If you disagree, listen again.

Frances Boyd:	I wanted to ask you about your company, Akzo. What's distinctive about Akzo in the chemical industry? What do you think makes it successful?
John Behan:	Akzo is the twelfth-largest chemical company in the world. And it's a chemical conglomerate, which means it combines several chemically related industries into one major chemical company. What makes it distinctive? It combines a lot of business concepts, and many, many different small businesses into one major company. It's global in nature, and it's managed at the local level. Akzo has now begun to reorganize into business units, which will manage their own businesses at the lowest level and closest to the customer base, which means that the product will get to the marketplace a lot faster, without a lot of what we call red tape and corporate bureaucracy, which will make it more effective and probably a better-organized company. That's what makes it distinctive.
FB:	When did Akzo first become aware of environmental concerns? And, when did it first change its operations for environmental reasons?
JB:	I really don't know when it became aware of environmental concerns, but there was a great global awareness led by the United States and also other North American industries back in the early '70s. There was an environmental movement, if you will. In Europe, where Akzo is located, the EC, which is the European Community, began to adopt treaty-like provisions, which are voluntary and could be adopted or not adopted within a certain period of time. Back in the late '70s those began. I would say that the environmental awareness movement really came to fruition in the mid-to-late '70s.
	Akzo's operations? I would say Akzo's operations have always been environmentally aware because it makes good economic sense not to have to clean up something that you caused, which would then deplete your profits in some way.
FB:	We hear a lot these days about "sustainable business development." Could you explain what this means?

JB:	Sustainable business development is basically defined to mean we have a world of resources, and they are not infinite. And you must use them wisely in order to provide an economic base for your people to live and to sustain them, without forever jeopardizing the environment which produces these resources. Now, as I said, it's an ephemeral concept without real definition. I think common sense governs here. We know that you don't bury hazardous waste and expect it to disappear in the future. It stays. You don't bury nuclear waste and expect it to disappear. It stays. You have to deal with it at some time, so basically sustainable means sustainable to everyone, not only the economy but to the world at large.
FB:	How does the concept of sustainable business development affect Akzo?
JB:	That's a pretty broad question. I think, you know, we want to stay in business. We're in business for our stockholders. I mean, they invest in our company and they expect a return on that investment. Now let's talk about the concept of strict liability for the moment. *Strict liability* means that you have caused a very hazardous situation or dangerous situation, you've been dealing with the hazardous situation—for example, chemicals—you've negligently or intentionally disposed of these chemicals in a way that is illegal or does not make good sense and, in a way, the courts look at this as a reason to hold the person who causes this harm strictly liable. That's the concept of strict liability. You pay for all the damage you cause, all the way down the line.
FB:	Let me ask you, then, if you could outline for us some of the basic principles governing Akzo's environmental policy.
JB:	We comply with the laws as we see them written, literally. We are strictly liable for any damage caused by our noncompliance. We have an accountability regimen, if you will, and that's that each business unit manager is responsible for his environmental compliance efforts. And, it is part of his job description, it's part of his compensation review and part of just selling our product—that we will sell it in an environmentally conscious way. Now that does not mean that we are volunteers, either. We just do what the law requires as well as, probably, a little bit more. It makes good economic sense and it's highly competitive these days to be a little bit ahead of the game because this is the trend in the world—that we're becoming greener as time goes on, within the concept of what is sustainable. You have to make money, provide jobs, and stay in business.

Unit 10: Crosby Valve & Gage Company
Choosing a Latin American Manufacturing Base

You will hear an interview with Theodore Teplow, former president and chief executive officer of the Crosby Valve & Gage Company and a graduate of the Harvard Business School. He speaks with the author about the Crosby company's international experience. Not only does Crosby make the highest quality safety valves, but it also markets them successfully all over the world.

Read the questions. Then listen to the tape and write your answers. Compare your responses with those of a classmate. If you disagree, listen again.

Theodore Teplow:	Crosby got into the safety valve business in the 1870s, and realized that the scope of their marketing was limited in the United States. They basically needed to have the whole world, the whole industrial world as a marketing base if they were going to grow the market for their products sufficiently to warrant the investment that they were making. There was a lot of competition, believe it or not, in the field that they had entered back then, which was not only safety valves but what they called "steam specialties," all of the products that were required around steam engines. When you see the year 1884 and you think of the development of the steam engine . . . , the steam engine grew both in Europe and the United States, and they went wherever the steam engines were used.

Frances Boyd:	If you think about your international markets again, can you think of any particular failures or bad experiences?
TT:	Oh, yes. I mean nothing is 100 percent, and in many cases we didn't pick the right partners. We had a, I would say, a dramatic failure in Mexico where we started with a joint venture and the managers that were our partners there just didn't manage it successfully. And it kept requiring additional investment from the United States until it became totally economically unviable and we closed it down. In Australia, we had a successful licensee that had been a family business that sold out to a company that was subsequently merged with another company. And in all the subsequent managerial changes, the attention that was put on our product line kept diminishing. And eventually we converted that manufacturing license back into just a sales representation, and then eventually even terminated that.
FB:	Thank you. I wonder how Crosby executives decide where to seek new markets? When you are entering a new part of the world, for example, what do you look at?
TT:	We're always looking for a situation where we can be the first one in. Because, if you can dominate a market, get the bulk of the market share, you quickly build up a base of product installed that has requirements for parts, sales, replacements, upgrade, repairs, service—what we call the *after market*—and those kinds of opportunities emerge from developing countries, when they go from a nonindustrial economy to an industrial economy.
FB:	And could you talk a little about how you, what role the relationship between the local contact and your company plays in your decision to enter a market?
TT:	Well, I have always felt personally, in my international business dealings, as has been the case in the country as well, that the most important decision you make is the person with whom you partner. You have to make certain that you have a similar philosophy about business ethics, that you certainly have to be certain that the partner has the technical competence to manufacture and market your products, to understand the developments that you're making and why they and how they function. And, you have to be certain that they're motivated to succeed.
FB:	And you feel you can find this out through research, through talking with the person?
TT:	You have to spend a lot of time one-on-one. Is this person going to be a good partner? It's like a marriage. You know, you wouldn't marry somebody that you didn't know for a few years.

Credits

Unit 1: Kentucky Fried Chicken
Exercise 1: Photos courtesy of Kentucky Fried Chicken Corporation.

Unit 2: Johnson & Johnson Consumer Products, Inc.
Exercise 1, 3: Photos courtesy of Johnson & Johnson Consumer Products, Inc.
Exercise 2: Interview with David Clare from the nationally broadcast public radio series, *The Corporate Conscience,* written and produced by David Freudberg, 1986. Used by permission.
Exercise 3A-1: Hollie, Pamela G. "Drug Rules Met on Time." Copyright © February 7, 1983. The New York Times Company, pp. D1 & D4. Reprinted by permission.
Exercise 3A-2, 3: "Tylenol's Miracle Comeback." Copyright October 17, 1983. Time Warner Inc. Reprinted by permission.
Exercise 7C: Credo courtesy of Johnson & Johnson. Used by permission.

Unit 3: Ben & Jerry's Homemade, Inc.
Exercise 1, 3: Photos courtesy of Ben & Jerry's Homemade, Inc.
Exercise 2: Tape and tapescript courtesy of Ben & Jerry's Homemade. Used by permission.
Exercise 3A-2: Seibert, Sam with Mac Margolis, "Hug a Tree, Kiss an Herb." *Newsweek*, May 1 ©1989. Newsweek, Inc. All rights reserved. Reprinted by permission.
Exercise 3A-3: "A Call to Pig Out for Peace." *Newsweek*, May 8 ©1989. Newsweek, Inc. All rights reserved. Reprinted by permission.
Exercise 7A: Letterhead courtesy of Ben & Jerry's Homemade, Inc. Used by permission.

Unit 4: Levi Strauss & Co.
Exercise 1, 3: Photos courtesy of Levi Strauss & Co. Drawing courtesey of Kazuaki Kora.
Exercise 3A-2, 3: Sevareid, Eric, "Finding the Fit," Ch. 5. *Enterprise.* NY: McGraw-Hill, 1984. Reprinted with permission of McGraw-Hill.

Unit 5: Stew Leonard's Dairy Store
Exercise 1, 3, 4: Photos courtesy of Stew Leonard's Dairy Store.
Exercise 2: Tape and tapescript courtesy of Stew Leonard's Dairy Store. Used by permission.
Exercise 3A-2, 3: Wald, Matthew. "Stew Leonard's, Believe It or Not!" Copyright © May 25, 1989 by The New York Times Company. Reprinted by permission.

Unit 6: Airbus Industrie, The Boeing Company
Exercise 1, 3: Photos courtesy of Airbus Industrie. Photos courtesy of The Boeing Company.
Exercise 2: Graph courtesy of *Fortune* magazine, ©1989. Used by permission.

Unit 7: Kidselebration, Inc.
Exercise 1, 3: Logo and photos courtesy of Kidselebration. Used by permission.
Exercise 2: Music courtesy of Kidselebration, ©1986. Used by permission.
Tape and tapescript courtesy of Deborah and Peter Roth. Used by permission.

Unit 8: Akzo n.v.
Exercise 1, 3: Photos courtesy of Akzo n.v.
Exercise 2: Tape and tapescript courtesy of John Behan. Used by permission.
Exercise 3B: Chart courtesy of Akzo n.v. Used by permission.
Exercise 7C: Akzo environmental policy document courtesy of Akzo n.v. Used by permission.

Unit 9: Perdue Farms, Inc.
Exercise 1, 3: Photos courtesy of Perdue Farms, Inc.
Exercise 2: Questionnaire inspired by Gail Fingado, Jane Kenefick.
Exercise 3A-2, 3: Reprinted by permission; ©1987 Thomas Whiteside. Originally in *The New Yorker*. All rights reserved.
Exercise 4: Inspired by the work of Fairfid Caudle on cross-cultural values in advertising.
Exercise 7A: Storyboard art courtesy of Asako Kora, my former student. Used by permission. Storyboard format courtesy of Cecilia deWolf Stein.

Unit 10: Crosby Valve & Gage Company
Exercise 1, 3: Photos used by permission of Crosby Valve & Gage Company.
Exercise 2: Tape and tapescript courtesy of Theodore Teplow. Used by permission.